THE WAY
PEOPLE
LIVE

Life on an Israeli Kibbutz

by Linda Jacobs Altman

Lucent Books, P.O. Box 289011, San Diego, CA 92198-9011

Library of Congress Cataloging-in-Publication Data

Altman, Linda Jacobs, 1943-
    Life on an Israeli kibbutz / Linda Jacobs Altman.
      p.   cm. — (The way people live)
    Includes bibliographical references and index.
    Summary: Describes daily life in an Israeli commune and provides
a history of the kibbutz movement.
    ISBN 1-56006-328-9 (alk. paper)
    1. Kibbutzim—Juvenile literature. [1. Kibbutzim. 2. Israel—
Social life and customs.] I. Title. II. Series.
HX742.2.A3A38   1996
307.77'6—dc20   95-38177
                                                       CIP
                                                       AC

Contents

FOREWORD
Discovering the Humanity in Us All   6

INTRODUCTION
A New Way of Living   8

CHAPTER ONE
The First Kibbutz   11

CHAPTER TWO
Work All Day, Dance the Hora All Night   20

CHAPTER THREE
Children of the Dream   34

CHAPTER FOUR
The Kibbutz and Its Arab Neighbors   46

CHAPTER FIVE
The New Kibbutz: A Community in Transition   58

CHAPTER SIX
Community Values, Personal Needs   70

CONCLUSION
The Kibbutz as Social Model   81

Notes   85
For Further Reading   88
Works Consulted   89
Index   91
Picture Credits   94
About the Author   95

Discovering the Humanity in Us All

The Way People Live series focuses on pockets of human culture. Some of these are current cultures, like the Eskimos of the Arctic; others no longer exist, such as the Jewish ghetto in Warsaw during World War II. What many of these cultural pockets share, however, is the fact that they have been viewed before, but not completely understood.

To really understand any culture, it is necessary to strip the mind of the common notions we hold about groups of people. These stereotypes are the archenemies of learning. It does not even matter whether the stereotypes are positive or negative; they are confining and tight. Removing them is a challenge that's not easily met, as anyone who has ever tried it will admit. Ideas that do not fit into the templates we create are unwelcome visitors—ones we would prefer remain quietly in a corner or forgotten room.

The cowboy of the Old West is a good example of such confining roles. The cowboy was courageous, yet soft-spoken. His time (it is always a he, in our template) was spent alternatively saving a rancher's daughter from certain death on a runaway stagecoach, or shooting it out with rustlers. At times, of course, he was likely to get a little crazy in town after a trail drive, but for the most part, he was the epitome of inner strength. It is disconcerting to find out that the cowboy is human, even a bit childish. Can it really be true that cowboys would line up to help the cook on the trail drive grind coffee, just hoping he would give them a little stick of pep-permint candy that came with the coffee shipment? The idea of tough cowboys vying with one another to help "Coosie" (as they called their cooks) for a bit of candy seems silly and out of place.

So is the vision of Eskimos playing video games and watching MTV, living in prefab housing in the Arctic. It just does not fit with what "Eskimo" means. We are far more comfortable with snow igloos and whale blubber, harpoons and kayaks.

Although the cultures dealt with in Lucent's The Way People Live series are often historically and socially well known, the emphasis is on the personal aspects of life. Groups of people, while unquestionably affected by their politics and their governmental structures, are more than those institutions. How do people in a particular time and place educate their children? What do they eat? And how do they build their houses? What kinds of work do they do? What kinds of games do they enjoy? The answers to these questions bring these cultures to life. People's lives are revealed in the particulars and only by knowing the particulars can we understand these cultures' will to survive and their moments of weakness and greatness.

This is not to say that understanding politics does not help to understand a culture. There is no question that the Warsaw ghetto, for example, was a culture that was brought about by the politics and social ideas of Adolf Hitler and the Third Reich. But the Jews who were crowded together in the ghetto cannot be understood by the Reich's politics. Their life was a day-to-day battle for existence, and the creativity and methods they used to prolong their lives is a vital story of human perseverance that would be denied by focusing only on the institutions of Hitler's Germany. Knowing that children as young as five or six outwitted Nazi guards on a daily basis, that Jewish policemen helped the Germans control the ghetto, that children attended secret schools in the ghetto and even earned diplomas—these are the things that reveal the fabric of life, that can inspire, intrigue, and amaze.

Books in the The Way People Live series allow both the casual reader and the student to see humans as victims, heroes, and onlookers. And although humans act in ways that can fill us with feelings of sorrow and revulsion, it is important to remember that "hero," "predator," and "victim" are dangerous terms. Heaping undue pity or praise on people reduces them to objects, and strips them of their humanity.

Seeing the Jews of Warsaw only as victims is to deny their humanity. Seeing them only as they appear in surviving photos, staring at the camera with infinite sadness, is limiting, both to them and to those who want to understand them. To an object of pity, the only appropriate response becomes "Those poor creatures!" and that reduces both the quality of their struggle and the depth of their despair. No one is served by such two-dimensional views of people and their cultures.

With this in mind, the The Way People Live series strives to flesh out the traditional, two-dimensional views of people in various cultures and historical circumstances. Using a wide variety of primary quotations—the words not only of the politicians and government leaders, but of the real people whose lives are being examined—each book in the series attempts to show an honest and complete picture of a culture removed from our own by time or space.

By examining cultures in this way, the reader will notice not only the glaring differences from his or her own culture, but also will be struck by the similarities. For indeed, people share common needs—warmth, good company, stability, and affirmation from others. Ultimately, seeing how people really live, or have lived can only enrich our understanding of ourselves.

A New Way of Living

To the casual observer, an Israeli kibbutz looks like any other successful and reasonably prosperous farming village. The buildings are modest but well constructed, the people seem happy, the land is green and good. Nothing identifies the kibbutz as perhaps the most successful experiment in collective living the world has ever seen.

A Peaceful Country Village

Most kibbutzim are laid out in a hub pattern, with public facilities at the center, residences in the next layer, and fields, factories, and offices on the outer rim. The centerpiece of the village is the dining hall, which serves as a gathering place for the whole community. Nearby are domestic and personal services—the laundry, shoe repair, sewing room, and barbershop—as well as a school that is attended by all the community's children.

One of the most popular styles of residence on the modern kibbutz is the garden apartment, with its own small yard and sleeping porch. These days, every apartment is likely to have a TV, a stereo, and at least a portable air conditioner.

Agriculture and Industry

Generally, a mix of agricultural, industrial, and commercial enterprises makes up the kibbutz's outer rim. Modern kibbutzim operate a wide range of businesses, from plastics factories to catering services, resort hotels, and law firms.

Though nonagricultural enterprises are now accepted in the kibbutz, they are recent additions to the economic base of the community. The earliest kibbutzim were strictly agricultural collectives. Their idea of diversification was growing several different crops so that a single failure would not jeopardize the livelihoods of everyone in the kibbutz.

Although commercial and industrial enterprises are now common on the kibbutz, farming remains a way of life for many kibbutzniks.

Through hard work and determination, the pioneers of the kibbutz created a thriving agricultural community in the barren desert of Palestine.

Modern kibbutzim have continued the practice of mixed farming. It is not uncommon to see orange and grapefruit orchards growing near lush vineyards and neatly planted rows of green vegetables. Some kibbutzim raise poultry, some keep dairy cattle and goats. Some grow flowers that are shipped to European florists in refrigerated containers.

With this variety and concentration of activities, today's kibbutz is a busy place. In the mornings, adults rush off to work and children head for school, much as they do in any American town. The main difference is that no one has to commute on a crowded freeway, or fight impatient crowds to catch a bus or train. People who work in the outer fields may use a motor scooter to get there and take their lunches along, but even they are within ten or fifteen minutes of home.

When the day's work is done, a kibbutz also resembles any other town. On a night when no special activity is planned, parents and children gather in their individual apartments to relax and socialize. Outside, some residents stroll quietly along well-kept pathways.

A Special Way of Life

These very modern conditions do not reveal the complex political history of the kibbutz. For most of its history, the kibbutz was a unique social experiment.

Today's kibbutzim are descended from a grand experiment begun in 1909 by Jews escaping the pogroms (mass murders) of Russia and eastern Europe. They went to Palestine, the land of their forefathers, to build a cooperative agricultural community, envisioning a place in which all members would be equal and all would share in the great work of turning a desert into a garden. They accomplished all this and more, building thriving communities that earned the respect and admiration of people all over the world.

Original residents owned no property, nor did they receive pay for their work. Even the clothes they wore came from a central storehouse and were returned to a central laundry. They lived in cramped rooms with no kitchen and no private bathroom, ate their

A Special Way of Life

In her book My Father, His Daughter, *Yaël Dayan, daughter of Israeli general Moshe Dayan, tells of the rhythms of a life lived close to the land.*

"My grandparents came to Palestine from the Ukraine, soon after the turn of the century, and settled . . . where the Jordan River flows south of Lake Tiberias [another name for the Sea of Galilee]. There they founded Deganya [Degania], the first kibbutz, where my father, Moshe, was born, less than a year after the First World War began. Most people on this globe are born, live, and die within a few miles' diameter. The roots are where the home is, where the grave is, where some of the children are to live and be buried. . . . I was born on the Hill of Moreh, lived in Nahalal, and will be returned to Shimron—overlooking it. My father was born in Deganya, grew up in Hahalal, and despite the long, complex, eventful, and rich route his life followed, he was returned, as he wished, to rest near where the roots are. The reclaimed land, the fertile valley, the Bedouin herds, the droughts were his home territory."

meals in a communal dining hall, and valued nothing so much as hard, physically punishing work. Children slept in separate houses away from their parents.

In the last years of the twentieth century, kibbutzim face a whole new set of challenges. The collective life the founders cherished is being replaced by private property and personal ambition. Parents and children live together in spacious apartments with individual kitchens and private bathrooms. Some kibbutzim have Olympic-size swimming pools, tennis courts, and fully equipped health clubs.

Leadership has passed from the founding generation to their children and grandchildren, who are constantly redefining what it means to be a kibbutznik. This process worries some of the older members; they wonder if a kibbutz can still be a kibbutz if industry replaces agriculture and members own cars, refrigerators, and TV sets. Shmuel Hadash, seventy years old and kibbutz-born, was harsh and outspoken in an interview with political commentator Yossi Melman:

I have no more illusions. . . . The kibbutz as an idea is dead. Its ideology has failed. . . . [The first kibbutzniks] tried to change human nature and create a new man. To my regret, the kibbutz did not succeed in this task, because man's nature is stronger than his deeds. In the kibbutz, as in any other human society, people like to sow little and reap the most.[1]

Others clearly disagree: A seventy-year-old kibbutznik named Meream Goldberger says:

When I came here [in 1944] there were just two trees. Look around. We built a village, we created a society that has lasted for decades. People around here say the kibbutz is dying? Well, people in this dying kibbutz are still living, and pretty well, too.[2]

Between these extremes lie many shades of opinion, but everyone agrees that the kibbutz movement faces a future of challenge and change. What will happen to this way of life?

1 The First Kibbutz

Israel's first kibbutz was built by Jewish men and women who endured prejudice and harsh discrimination in Russia and eastern Europe. They had been segregated in impoverished neighborhoods, barred from many professions, even forbidden to own land. As an isolated and easily identifiable minority, they were vulnerable to the murderous violence of sudden and unprovoked pogroms, or organized massacres.

From Victims to Pioneers

Between 1881 and 1903, pogroms wiped out entire Jewish communities; men, women, and children were cut down in the streets, whole villages were put to the torch. Many Jews fled this horror to build a new life in Palestine, historic home of their ancestors.

Though Palestine was the birthplace of the Jewish religion, the first refugees did not go there for religious reasons. They had abandoned the beliefs and practices of Judaism for more secular philosophies, and the society they created reflected political rather than religious values.

As socialists, they believed that the community as a whole should own all property and distribute it among the members according to need. Each member was expected to do his or her share of the work and participate fully in the life of the community. There would be no privileged elite exploiting the working class for its own gain. There would be only comrades living and working together in absolute equality.

As Zionists, the immigrants wanted to create a Jewish homeland that would someday take its place in the community of nations. Zionists believed that an independent nation was the only solution to anti-Semitism, or the hatred and persecution of Jews. They believed Jews would always be in danger so long as they were an unwanted minority scattered over many nations, with no political power or national identity.

The blending of these two philosophies led first to the *kvutza*, a small, familylike group that worked together and shared expenses. By hiring themselves out as a work crew on different farms, the members of the *kvutza* earned a living and mastered farming practices at the same time.

A Place Called Cornflower

In 1909, the *kvutza* acquired a 750-acre tract of land on the western shore of the Sea of Galilee, near the Jordan River. They received this land from the Jewish National Fund, a Zionist group that bought it from absentee Arab owners. The agreement between the *kvutza* and JNF was simple. The settlers would clear the land and cultivate it. When they produced a salable crop, they would pay a percentage of the net profit as rent. The jubilant pioneers called their new home Degania, Hebrew for the hardy blue cornflower that grew wild over its hills.

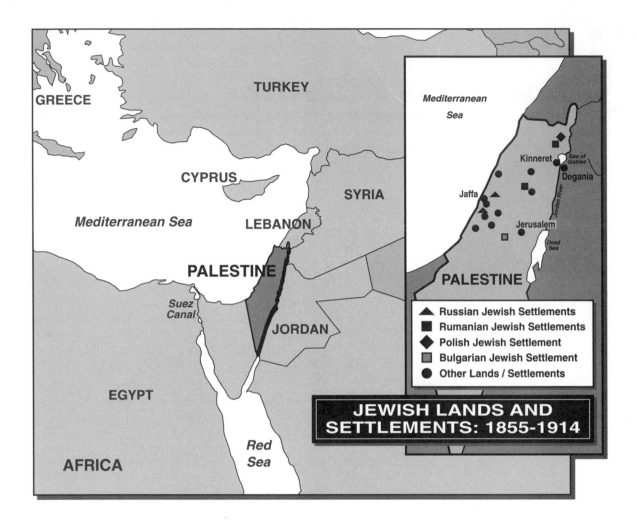

JEWISH LANDS AND SETTLEMENTS: 1855-1914

Russian Jewish Settlements
Rumanian Jewish Settlements
Polish Jewish Settlement
Bulgarian Jewish Settlement
Other Lands / Settlements

On October 28, 1910, ten men and two women took possession of temporary quarters in the abandoned Arab village of Um Juni, which was near the property but not on it. JNF had made arrangements to build a permanent village for them, but until it was ready Um Juni would have to serve.

The Challenge of Equality

In keeping with their socialist ideals, the settlers immediately abolished private property. They agreed that competition, personal ambition, and status seeking had no place in their new community. They aspired instead to *ezra hadadit*, or mutual aid, in all things, sharing equally in the hardships, the work, and the benefits of group life.

From the beginning, they stressed the idea that "equal" did not mean "all alike." A collective that tried to stamp out individual differences would soon become harsh and dictatorial. A commune should not be based upon repression and gray conformity: To be healthy and vital, it should not only tolerate differences but actually encourage them, as founding member Joseph Bussel noted in his reminiscences of Degania's early days:

I never thought that the pattern of kvutza life [would wipe out] the disposition of the member. . . . I continue to be of the opinion that the kvutza should conduct a tolerance of different views. . . . I consider it as a victory for our principles if people so different from each other are able to live together . . . without any serious conflicts between us.[3]

There was conflict, of course, but also tolerance and a vibrant sense of community. Harsh though conditions sometimes were, the original members of Degania would one day recall the pioneering days as a time of immense satisfaction. Everyone worked together, lived together, and played together, creating the group solidarity and sense of community that would become their legacy to future generations.

One of that original group summed up the challenge of transforming a wasteland into a working farm: "[T]he land had lost its fertility and it seemed to us that we ourselves, divorced from it, had become barren in spirit. Now we must give it our strength and give it back its creativeness."[4]

Reclaiming the Land

Making the land fertile again required all the knowledge, strength, and ingenuity the settlers could muster. Even the climate seemed to be against them, as political scientist Mark Tessler makes clear in his discussion of the early kibbutz: "Two hundred meters below sea level, Degania was exceedingly hot during the long summers, with temperatures above 100 degrees for extended periods. Also, as elsewhere in Palestine, diseases, especially malaria, were common at this time."[5]

Degania was covered with swamps where malaria-bearing mosquitoes and other dangerous organisms bred in pools of stagnant water. Until the settlers drained those swamps, malaria decimated their ranks. Nearly everyone caught it, suffering the high fevers, nausea, and delirium of periodic attacks. When too many people were sick at once, the pace of work slowed to a halt.

It soon became clear that a dozen sick and exhausted people could not hope to finish this task alone. Reluctantly, the kibbutzniks agreed to hire outside workers. The prospect of becoming employers went against their ideals of equal participation and return to the soil, but they saw no other choice. With the survival of their community at stake, the Deganians came to terms with their ideals by hiring fellow Jews and treating them as comrades and equals for the duration of their employment.

When the land was cleared and ready to plant, the Jewish National Fund supplied seed for the first crop and money to live on until the first harvest. The Deganians bought six mules and two horses from nearby farmers and used them to haul water from the Jordan

Working together, the settlers of Degania endured harsh conditions while trying to transform the barrenness of Palestine into a working farm.

River. All that was left to do was decide what crops to plant. As field-workers in a roving *kvutza*, the comrades were skilled in tending crops, but not in land use and planning. Questions of what to grow, and where and when to grow it, remained a mystery.

After discussing the problem at length, the novice farmers planted tomatoes and potatoes, which failed because neither would grow in Degania's soil and climate. To become successful farmers, the kibbutzniks had to learn which crops were suited to the local environment, such as eggplant, okra, and squash, and how to rotate those crops to keep the soil fertile. In the early days they grew barely enough for their own needs, with nothing left over to sell. The same Zionist groups which provided the land also helped with operating expenses until the kibbutz became self-sustaining.

Living Conditions

In the evenings, the Deganians gathered to share a meager meal and discuss work assignments or any other work problems. When that was finished, they danced—always the hora, a whirling, circling folk dance in which everyone linked arms and abandoned private concerns to the joy of the moment. The music that moved them came from the tradition of the Hasidim, a devout Jewish sect who were known for their exuberant music and dancing. Years later, founding member Miriam Baratz could still recall those nightly gatherings:

> After a day of hard and grinding labour we would sit in a circle, begin with romantic songs, pour out our heart, and then go over to Hassidic tunes which bring all of us to our feet dancing, and perspiring. . . . My friends' remembrance of their somewhat hysterical dancing away the night, as an anodyne [pain reliever] to the never-removed fatigue of the day's work, stirs [sympathy and admiration]. . . . Deathly weary we would lie down to sleep, but the biting mosquitoes would not let us sleep.[6]

Not even horas and Hasidic music could relieve the grim and cheerless environment

The founding members of Degania were faced with many hardships. In addition to learning new farming techniques, kibbutzniks were forced to change their diets and live without even the most basic comforts.

in which the Deganians lived, however. They had to learn how to do without even the most basic comforts of life. They got used to living without running water, indoor toilets, or proper beds, but they had a more difficult time adjusting to the change in their diets. Instead of old favorites, which would have been expensive and time-consuming to prepare, Degania's menu relied on local produce. Russians who were accustomed to blintzes and borscht found themselves eating eggplant, okra, and lentils—and not liking it at all.

According to Miriam Baratz, who served as one of the cooks, "Not a small quantity of these foods were secretly thrown under the table. . . . But there were never any quarrels about food. The occasional differences were about quite different subjects."[7]

For the two years that the pioneers lived in Um Juni, it was impossible to stay clean or to care for dishes and cooking utensils in a hygienic way. The amenities of civilized living would have to wait for the day when their permanent village was ready for occupancy.

When that day finally came, the first kibbutzniks found that a lot of old problems moved with them to their new quarters. A terse journal entry from the time touches on some of the continuing areas of concern:

The new buildings are being occupied; the working conditions in the kitchen have improved a little; but the food is as sparse and as monotonous as before. . . . [O]ne hears the complaints about the dissatisfaction of the women members. . . . [They] are accused of being wasteful; and . . . they do not keep the produce in a desirable form.[8]

"Women's Work"

These observations come from a time when women were trying to redefine their role

The "Jewish Problem"

The emerging kibbutz lifestyle was in part a reaction to the rootlessness of a people who belonged nowhere and so were forced to live anywhere the majority population would accept—or at least tolerate—their presence. Dan Leon touches on this in his book The Kibbutz: A New Way of Life.

"Here were a people lacking any connection with the soil, with agriculture, and with nature, divorced from the primary means of production both rural and urban. Tolerated as long as the host nations were in need of the . . . economic functions which the Jews performed in trade and commerce . . . they were the natural scapegoats in periods of instability and upheaval. . . . Lacking the possibility as well as the desire to assimilate because of their uniqueness, the Jewish masses were at best able to transfer the Jewish problem from place to place, but never to solve it. The only . . . permanent solution lay in the territorial concentration of this scattered people, yet this, too, would be [ineffective] unless accompanied by a social transformation. . . . The normalisation and stabilisation of Jewish life demanded . . . a return to the land, to agriculture and to physical labour. This was the only outlet which offered a prospect of tackling the Jewish anomaly [difference] at its roots."

within the kibbutz. In the beginning, it had seemed entirely natural for men to work in the fields and women to do the sewing, cooking, and cleaning. In time, the women began to resent this arrangement. They had not come to Palestine to spend their days in an endless round of housekeeping chores. They had come to be pioneers and equals, to live and work close to the land, creating a community that was rich and varied enough to include everyone. Equality, after all, was the very foundation of kibbutz life.

The women complained, and to their credit the men made an effort to include them in the income-producing work of the community. "[T]he woman still had to fight for assignments in the agricultural branches," explained one early member of Degania, "but she finally won her battle."[9] Women took the lead in establishing and operating a successful dairy farm.

The birth of Degania's first children raised a whole new set of concerns. Once more the role of women became a topic of discussion as the settlers wrestled with the problem of how a cooperative community should care for its young. The traditional family structure, in which the mother stayed home and devoted herself to housekeeping and child care, was neither possible nor desirable in a pioneering community. The work of every member was necessary to the survival of the kibbutz, and the women themselves showed no desire to give up their jobs for full-time motherhood.

In 1917, the Deganians decided that child rearing would become a communal project, just like everything else in their society. Kibbutzniks generally credit Joseph Bussel for the idea. Said Joseph Baratz:

[He] was the father of the conception of joint bringing-up and education of children. Bussel pressed for the adoption of the principle of joint care of the children at the expense of the entire community.

Since it would free the woman-mother, who could be used for other kinds of work, the child would know only about the co-operative way of life.[10]

The kibbutz assigned one woman to care for all the children, and put aside a house where she and her charges could spend the day while the mothers worked. The children spent the night in their parents' quarters. Other kibbutzim would expand the concept into twenty-four-hour group homes where children lived with age-mates and a caretaker. Degania never adopted that practice. Children ate, played, studied, and worked away from their parents, but they slept at home.

Belonging to Degania

In the early days, Degania was open and unstructured, with no special requirement for membership, no formal process of making application. People came to throw in their lot with the kibbutz, and so the commune grew. Joseph Baratz explained:

Anybody who considered himself part of us . . . remained and he was a member. We did not ask him to accept a creed. There were no elected committees. The vatikim [founding members], acquainted with the economy and pattern of life, deliberated about every small and large matter, and decided to act. Of course they were always glad to listen to the members' advice.[11]

Accommodating a growing population of Jews from different cultures was not easy. In 1910, a group of Zionist officials opened the door of immigration to several thousand Yemenites, Jews from the North African country of Yemen, whose customs and language the Europeans did not understand. Most were illiterate, lacking even the most basic education. To the Russian and European Jews who were well read, politically aware, and accustomed to Western standards regarding housekeeping, personal hygiene, and social conduct, the Yemenites were a shock. They seemed more like Arab peasants than Jewish pioneers.

Dozens of them settled near Degania. Said one pioneer member:

They live with us and are wage workers. The conditions of their life are most difficult. They have large families, including aged parents. We have urged the institutions to build houses for them on Jewish National Fund land with small plots which they could cultivate. . . . These are not workers whom we have invited to lighten our burden. . . . [T]hey come to us from Judah and other places to work, to breathe the free air and to relax from their worries and stress. But they consider

Without any special requirements for membership in the early days of Degania, Jews from many different cultures joined the growing kibbutz.

this . . . as their home for life—their future.[12]

A small group of members believed that the Yemenite workers should be fully included in the life of the kibbutz. To do less would be exploitation of labor. The majority argued that the Yemenites simply did not have the training to participate in discussions and decisions about economic or social issues. Including them would be a mistake.

There were no established rules or guidelines to help the Deganians decide the issue, no set procedures for resolving the conflict. Like most everything else in the kib-butz, the members had to figure it out as they went along. This time the issue was not settled successfully. Despite lengthy and impassioned discussions, the two factions could not come to an agreement. Those who could not accept the decision to exclude the Yemenites organized themselves into a more-or-less formal opposition. Eventually, all of them left Degania.

A Heritage of Jewish Tradition

Shaping the character of their community was important to the Deganians. Together,

they decided what language they would speak and what traditions they would observe. Members came to the kibbutz speaking two languages: the native tongue of their former homeland, and at least a smattering of Yiddish (a blend of Hebrew and medieval German, spoken by most European Jews). Thanks to Yiddish, Russians, Poles, Hungarians, and others were able to communicate with one another. They purposely avoided Hebrew, the ancestral language of the Jewish people. In this, the Deganians were out of step with the rest of the Yishuv (Jewish community) in Palestine. A growing group of Zionists wanted to make Hebrew the principal language of the land.

The Deganians did not like that idea at all. To them, Hebrew was the language of the synagogue, useful for prayers, perhaps, but not for buying fertilizer and tractor parts in town, or arguing the political issues of the day. As socialists, many Deganians rejected Hebrew and anything else that reminded them of religion. The few Jewish traditions they followed, out of sentiment or habit, were adapted to their secular (nonreligious) lifestyle.

When some members wanted to begin limited observance of the Sabbath (the "day of rest" in Jewish tradition, from sundown on Friday to sundown on Saturday), the most ardent socialists argued against it. Limited observance of some annual holidays might be permissible, they said, but Sabbath came every week. Even a watered-down observance would interfere with kibbutz routine.

Others disagreed, and so in true kibbutz fashion, the membership voted. It was the will of the majority that Sabbath be set aside as a day on which only the most essential work would be done. Everyone was pleasant-ly surprised by the results of their secularized Sabbath observance. People rested without feeling guilty and enjoyed neglected intellectual pursuits. Sabbath worked so well as a stress reducer and safety valve that the community began holding its general assembly on Saturday nights, with a membership rested in body and calm in mind, ready to deliberate on the problems facing the community.

In their third year, the Deganians finally decided to follow the general trend and make Hebrew the official language of their kibbutz. The decision sent many members scurrying to find classes and lesson materials so they could do their part in reviving the ancient language of Eretz Israel (the land of Israel).

The Legacy of Degania

Despite conflicts, self-doubts, and occasional blunders, the Deganians managed to do what they had set out to do: establish a collective society where people could live and work together for the good of all. Some fifty years after the founding of Degania, one of the vatikim summed up its accomplishments with quiet pride:

> Was our life perfection? Certainly not. We are all flesh and blood. [In Degania] we carried out the first experiment (in Palestine) of integral co-operative life.... And fortunate we are . . . that we are not alone and that there are hundreds of kvutzot and kibbutzim, that tens of thousands of Jews live an integrated co-operative life. But all this is not our work. The plough ploughed; the seeder sowed and the builder built.[13]

Work All Day, Dance the Hora All Night

As the kibbutz movement grew, individual settlements banded together to sponsor youth groups and educational programs all over the Jewish world. Three secular federations spread the kibbutz philosophy, along with one that attempted to blend socialism and Orthodox Judaism into a meaningful way of life. This religious group, called Hakibbutz Hadati, generally limited its recruiting operations to Orthodox neighborhoods.

Kibbutzniks represented a new and more vigorous Jewish identity: joyous, sunburned pioneers who spent their days revitalizing the land and their nights dancing wild horas around a blazing fire. Like most legends, this perception was highly romanticized, but it was exactly what Zionist groups needed to recruit young people to the cause.

Natural Hazards

Once they arrived at their new homes, romantic images gave way to hard facts. Recruits encountered conditions in some ways similar to those that greeted the first kibbutzniks. Malaria remained a threat wherever there was swampland to drain, and other problems plagued settlers in every region.

In the desert near the Syrian border, for example, kibbutzniks faced *chamseen*, literally "fifty" in Arabic, meaning that there would be about fifty hot, dry days in a year.

Although life on the kibbutz was romanticized by outsiders, a kibbutznik's day was often consumed by endless hours spent revitalizing the settlement's land.

It was not an ordinary heat, this *chamseen*. It was a desert heat that stuck like dust in your nostrils and was so thick you felt you could lie back on it. You could not work in it, unless you and probably several generations before you had been born in it.[14]

An even more unbearable hazard was the *barhash*, an incredible mass of mosquitoes, gnats, and sand flies that made summers miserable. Golda Meir, who served as prime minister of Israel in the sixties and early seventies, never forgot her futile efforts to cope with *barhash* during her time as a member of Kibbutz Merhavia:

In the summer we went to work at four in the morning because it was impossible to stay in the fields when the sun came up because of the *barhash*. . . . We used to smear ourselves with Vaseline, when we had it, wear high collars and long sleeves, wrap ourselves in kerchiefs, and come home with the *barhash* stuck in our eyes, ears, and nostrils. Even the cows used to stampede in the fields when the *barhash* came out. I had a solution for all my other problems, but not for the *barhash*.[15]

Putting Down Roots

In spite of these harsh conditions, kibbutzniks loved the land they farmed. They felt linked to it because they worked it, not because they owned it. Kibbutzniks rejected all property rights as a matter of principle. Lands belonging to everybody in general because it belonged to nobody in particular suited their purposes.

"National ownership of land," wrote author Melford Spiro, "[avoids] such 'evils' as land speculation, absentee ownership, and 'unearned' income through rent. Moreover, it prevents the rise of a society composed of a landed gentry and a disinherited peasantry."[16]

To the pioneer, land by its very nature was sacred, as one lifelong kibbutznik explained:

People returned to this country, poverty-stricken, without a government or any national organization, with the sole idea of settling the land. They were not to become merchants or bankers as their ancestors had been. . . . [W]henever a kibbutz was started, it received its most valuable gift from the nation: the soil. . . . [N]either man nor the land can be subjugated: They are forever free; they cannot become private property since they belong to God. This principle . . . has found its finest realization in the fact that a kibbutz doesn't own its land, but cultivates it as a gift from the nation.[17]

With hopes of settling and cultivating the land, Russian Jews make the long trek to Palestine during the 1930s. These pioneers believed the land was sacred and not subject to private ownership.

Share and Share Alike

The rule against private property did not stop with land. It extended to everything, even clothing and small personal items. In the early days, zealous socialists sometimes went overboard to eliminate private ownership from their collective lives, enforcing the ban on property strictly and without exception. One longtime kibbutznik recalled the pain and shock of new members, forced to give up treasured possessions:

> [I]t was terribly hard, terribly cruel. . . . It's impossible to fathom the difficulty of the initial adjustment [new people] were required to make. I have no words to describe it. You just came—and you found yourself at storehouse A. This was a clothes storehouse to which you submitted everything you owned—every single thing, from shoelaces to whatever, and on Friday you came in and received from the stock clerk a package of clothing for the coming week—whatever she had arranged for you. This was storehouse A, a total commune. So imagine people coming from abroad, from wealthy homes, in expensive suits and dresses, and within a day everything was taken away from them. Even I, who knew what to expect, remember this feeling. When I joined the kibbutz my parents, who worried about me, supplied me with all the best. They bought me a new leather coat, and on my back I carried a new bed and mattress, walking all the way from the train station, several kilometers away. A day later—not a sign of it was left for me. Everything became common property—out of which you get what you are assigned. I who was prepared for this, reacted in a relatively moderate way; but the newcomers who arrived from abroad—it broke them down, ruined them. It depressed them terribly, storehouse A.[18]

Gifts from outside the kibbutz created a particularly sensitive problem. In theory, anything a member received from well-meaning relatives and friends was to be turned over to the community. Some people resented that policy, especially regarding gifts that were small, personal, and held great sentimental value. Even pioneers who gladly worked land they did not own, and never complained about the hardship and poverty of their lives, could get testy when a favorite sweater was declared the property of the kibbutz.

For the Good of the Collective

These discontents notwithstanding, those who wanted to liberalize the rules regarding personal property could not muster enough support for their position. The prospect of making exceptions came with too many uncertainties about who would draw the line, where it would fall, and how many people might end up on the wrong side of it. To the kibbutzniks of the twenties and thirties, achieving the communal ideal was more important than flexibility about the rules that governed their lives.

The most important rule of all was the one that required every member to place the welfare of the collective ahead of his own. This emphasis on the group was revealed in every aspect of kibbutz living, from the decision-making process and the emphasis on *ezra hadadit* to the constant presence of other people.

One longtime kibbutznik offered an example of such forced interaction and the toll it can take on the individual:

The emphasis on the group forced kibbutzniks to place the welfare of the collective before their own. As a result, kibbutzniks forfeited privacy to live and work communally.

In the city, if you have a fight with a business colleague, it's not so bad; you only see him during business hours anyway. But here you have a fight with a chaver [member], and he is more than a business colleague. He's a chaver of the kibbutz; he's your friend, and you must live with him and see him every day. It's not pleasant.[19]

Putting the group first meant learning to live without privacy. A person who wanted to be alone a good deal of the time became an object of suspicion and distrust. Psychiatrist Bruno Bettelheim discovered this during the time he lived on a kibbutz:

My photographer-companion could not accustom himself to how kibbutzniks feel free to walk in on him at any hour of the day or night, no matter what he was occupied with. Eventually both of us, who had initially liked the idea of living in a true community, felt a . . . need to escape for a few hours to the anonymity of city life, where we could for moments be ourselves; where we were not expected to want to be always with others.

What made it so hard was that this longing for a bit of privacy, which to us seemed so natural, was felt by others to be a deliberate shunning of their company. It was not so much that others were so intrusive—this was true only for a small minority; most kibbutzniks we found very considerate. Our dilemma was that they so obviously meant well but were truly offended if we wanted some time to ourselves.[20]

Governing the Community

Like the Deganians who preceded them, later kibbutzniks held endless meetings to determine matters of policy and procedure. These discussions could become heated, and sometimes overlong. Every member was

The Group Ideal

In Kibbutz: Venture in Utopia, *Melford E. Spiro discussed the importance of group values in kibbutz society. According to Spiro, this focus on the collective is more than an abstract philosophy of the kibbutzim; it is a way of life.*

"The emphasis on the moral value of the group means . . . that group living and group experiences are valued more highly than their individual counterparts. Indeed, so important is the value of group experience that those [members] who seek a great degree of privacy are viewed as [odd]. The kibbutz is interested in creating a chevra [community]. The ultimate criterion of either a good kibbutz, a good high school, or a good kindergarten, is whether or not it has become a chevra. The term, chevra, literally denotes a society; but its connotation . . . is a group which is characterized by intimacy and interaction, and by mutual concern, if not by love. A chevra, in short, is . . . [an] 'organic community.' It is apparent, therefore, that . . . the person who cherishes his own privacy more than a group experience constitutes a threat to the group. His desire for privacy either prevents the group from becoming a chevra, or symbolizes the fact that it is not a chevra, for if it were, he would prefer to be with the group than to be alone."

---

entitled to have a say, and to gather support for a particular point of view. Once the matter came to a vote, however, the time for discussion and persuasion was over. Everyone was expected to accept the majority opinion with grace and good cheer, regardless of his or her personal feelings.

That informal system worked as long as the group was a small, familylike *kvutza*. When it grew to a large kibbutz with a population of perhaps three hundred, members had to be more inventive to insure that everyone had his or her say in the decision-making process. On every kibbutz, the weekly members' meeting, or general assembly, was the most important governing body.

In these lengthy sessions, members thrashed out everything from new policies and financial plans to acceptance of new members and personal requests from existing members. The strength of the general assembly was its total democracy; the weakness, its tendency to prolong discussion of even minor issues until the meeting bogged down in a morass of detail.

To streamline the decision-making process, most kibbutzim had a Secretariat, a type of executive council composed of the four top elective officers in the community: farm-manager, secretary, treasurer, and work-organizer. The Secretariat supervised the work of a wide range of committees, which dealt with every facet of kibbutz life, including economy, education, culture, festivals, political activity, health, recreation, and social life.

Neither the committees nor the Secretariat had authority over the general assembly, though the Secretariat had a certain moral authority to sway public opinion. As the executive body, it set the agenda for assembly meetings and researched issues in order to keep the membership informed.

To avoid creating a class distinction between the leaders and the followers, kibbutzim limited the terms of all elected officials and made sure they received no special privileges—not even a reduction in their work hours. The result was a government composed of people who served from a sense of duty rather than personal ambition.

Life in the Dining Hall

In this determinedly communal environment, no facility was more important than the dining hall. There the kibbutzniks came together for their communal meals and held celebrations, ceremonies, and general assemblies. Despite this acknowledged importance to community life, the earliest dining halls were bleak and utilitarian. A typical facility was noisy, with bare, whitewashed walls, long tables with paper placemats instead of cloths, and wooden benches instead of chairs. Kibbutz meals matched the surroundings: functional, hasty, and prepared with little attention to taste or appearance.

In this strictly utilitarian atmosphere, an inventive tossed salad became a staple of the diet. In time, the "kibbutz salad" became nearly as famous as hora dancing. American writer Michael Gorkin described his encounter with mealtime on a kibbutz:

The dining hall was almost empty when I arrived. A long, badly lit room with about seventy Formica tables, it had the capacity to seat all of Bilat's three hundred members as well as any volunteers, visitors or army reservists who happened to be around. On the average, I had been told, some fifty of these extras were generally there. Eating arrangements were informal, and in the evenings you could come as late as 8:00 P.M. and the tables would still have the tomatoes and cucumbers on them, and the kibbutznik wheeling around the eggs, herring and olives would still be there. . . . I began dicing up the vegetables and the hard-boiled egg into a salad—that celebrated kibbutz salad which you ate every breakfast and dinner as long as you were there, and which somehow should have become boring, and it did, but not so much as you

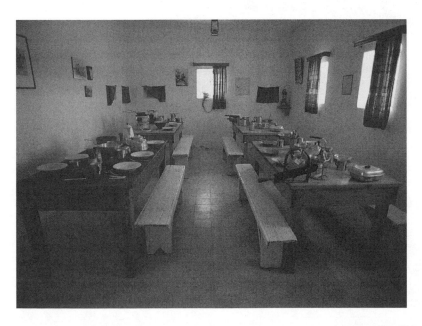

A reconstruction of the dining hall at Kibbutz Revivim as it appeared in 1947. Furnished with long wooden benches and whitewashed walls, the traditional dining hall has been described as "bleak and utilitarian."

Work All Day, Dance the Hora All Night **25**

expected. In fact, once you put the oil and vinegar on it, and mixed in a few olives and onions, it was . . . good.[21]

As the kibbutzim became better established, the atmosphere—and the food—improved, but with improvement came a certain rigidity in the way meals were prepared and served. Soon there were rules where none had been before. Sometimes these rules got in the way, as one kitchen worker discovered when she tried to make a small change in the method of food service:

When the first gong sounded it meant that the meal was ready. People came in at their leisure, and sat wherever they pleased. I . . . had to watch out for whoever had just sat down, and run with his or her tray of food. I ran all the time. Later I made a decision that people have to take their seats in a systematic fashion—starting from the corner table, filling all the seats around it, then starting at the next table, etc. This made our food serving somewhat more efficient. It was considered a radical change. [Then] I tried to install self-service meals in our dining room. This wasn't a decision we could make by ourselves in the kibbutz, so I went "upstairs," to the administration of the kibbutz movement, and I started to fight for the self-service system. The reaction I found, the opposition, was our familiar motto: "It will destroy the kibbutz.". . . Well, several years later, we did switch to self-service . . . by now, it's pretty clear that the kibbutz wasn't destroyed by this innovation.[22]

Kibbutzniks gather for a communal meal in their busy dining hall. Although the atmosphere of the dining hall improved over time, it continued to be governed by strict rules.

The Work You Love to Hate

The workload of an established kibbutz divided neatly into two categories: productive work, which yielded income, and "service" work, which did not. This second class included the laundry, the kitchen, and all children's services, jobs that have traditionally fallen to women.

Though all work was supposed to be equally valuable, domestic service simply did not carry the status of income-producing activity. Women especially went to great lengths to avoid it for fear of slipping back into their traditional domestic roles. The work itself was often just as physically demanding as the most strenuous agricultural labor, as a former laundry worker recalled:

> The laundry was a tin hut that didn't even have a sewage system for the water we used. There were some large boilers heated by wood. The clothes were scrubbed by hand, using special wooden boards, and then were put to rinse in another tank. To take them out, we had to turn over this rinsing tank, with all its contents. The water spilled out all over the floor and we just stood there, knee deep in water.[23]

Of all the jobs in the kibbutz, none was so dreaded as kitchen duty. Cooking, washing dishes, and serving food brought back memories of domesticity for the women and made the men feel impossibly clumsy, because they had never learned their way around a kitchen. The only fair way to staff food service positions was by a rotation system, in which everyone served their turn. Though this made the duty more bearable for all concerned, the rotation in many kibbutzim stopped short of treating men and women as

Although dreaded by both male and female kibbutzniks, kitchen duty—which included cooking, serving food, and washing dishes— was an important and demanding chore.

equals. Men served for a two- or three-month period, women for a year.

Because everyone had to serve at one time or another, being relegated to kitchen work did not affect a person's standing in the community. This was not the case with other low-status assignments, the worst of which was to become a *p'kak* (literally, "cork"), a perpetual substitute, who lacked the strength or skill for a regular work assignment. Author Melford Spiro explained:

> One day [the p'kak] may substitute for a sick person in the carpentry shop; another

Labor is greatly valued on the kibbutz. Regardless of whether a kibbutznik works in agriculture or domestic service, his or her workday is governed by rules and regulations that dictate working hours, rest breaks, overtime, and vacations.

day he may take the place of a vacationing shepherd, and so on. The kibbutz tries to avoid relegating anyone to the position of p'kak because of its demoralizing effect on the chaver. In a society in which labor is the highest value, a person who is formally recognized as having little working ability enjoys little prestige, and work-prestige is one of the important motives in the dynamics of the kibbutz economy.[24]

Rights and Responsibilities of Workers

In pioneering times, nobody worried much about managing workers. There was one rule: Start working when you get up and don't quit till the sun goes down. Only when the swamps were drained and the deserts irrigated did the kibbutzim begin to structure their working lives with rules and regulations.

A typical labor code reached into every aspect of the workplace, laying out regulations for working hours and rest breaks, overtime and holiday duty, vacations and leaves. People were expected to work eight hours a day in winter, nine in summer. All workers took midday rest/lunch periods of one hour in winter and two to three hours in the summer, when the scorching heat could make strenuous labor not only unbearable, but dangerous as well.

The provisions regarding annual leave (vacations) reveal a humanistic concern for the health, welfare, and morale of every worker: For example, newly married couples were entitled to "a honeymoon of six work days,[25] and grandparents could take off work three or four times a year to visit grandchildren who did not live on the kibbutz. No time off taken by new mothers during the year they gave birth was deducted from their annual leave allowance. Later, at the end of the period of breast-feeding their children, the rules provided that they "should have a week's complete rest at their home, and their respective annual leave should be debited with only three days."[26]

One interesting rule required workers to take their annual leaves away from the kibbutz, apparently in the belief that a change of scene was healthy for everyone. Vacation periods ranged from eight working days for members under thirty years old to sixteen days for those sixty and over.

The rules governing the workplace were based on the assumption that kibbutzniks found meaning in labor and therefore did not need to be motivated by external rewards, or threatened by external punishments. Each worker was a full partner in the economic life of the kibbutz, with the right to comment upon the rules before they were cast into final form. Because members worked under a code that they helped to create, there was a high degree of compliance and a minimum of complaint.

Cultural and Recreational Activities

Life was not all work and struggle. Once the kibbutzim had established themselves as successful communities, they made time for a variety of cultural and recreational activities. A typical activity schedule was so crowded that no one could possibly take part in everything:

> There is hardly an evening in the kibbutz without some form of cultural activity, mainly in the framework of special-interest circles. . . . Nearly every settlement has its own choir, orchestra, dramatic and folk-dancing circles, which reach exceptionally high performance standards. There are weekly or monthly

The Early Kibbutzim

In their study of kibbutz-born sabras, published in Twenty Years Later: Kibbutz Children Grown Up, *psychologists A. I. Rabin and Benjamin Beit-Hallahmi evaluated the long-term results of the communal lifestyle and discussed some of the reasons the first kibbutzniks chose this particular form of social organization.*

"There were particular circumstances that made the kibbutz such a success. . . . It was an ideal solution to the problem of colonizing Palestine in the years before the founding of the State of Israel. Settling the land with groups of young, vigorous, and idealistic individuals having attachments only to the collective was more practical and logical than settling through the traditional way of family homesteading. This form of settlement was also militarily more defensible, a fact worth considering given the hostile environment into which Zionist settlements entered. . . . The idea of a voluntary membership commune grew out of a combination of nationalist and socialist ideologies. . . . Agricultural work was seen as the way to changing the abnormal social structure of the Jews in the Diaspora [dispersion], and thus agricultural settlements became the instruments for resolving not only national problems but also human ones."

bulletins and papers. Visiting lecturers, from the kibbutzim and outside, cover almost every topic under the sun. Study-circles, generally led by a kibbutz member, devote themselves to topics which range from kibbutz theory to ancient and modern Jewish and general history, Marxism and sociology, literature and mathematics, education and philosophy . . . science and archaeology.[27]

Celebrations also played a big part in communal life: Like the Deganians in their famous "battle of the Sabbath," later kibbutzniks celebrated Jewish festivals and holidays as cultural rather than religious occasions. The age-old ceremonies were a link to the Jewish past and also to the timeless rhythms of life lived close to the land, from Passover in the spring when fields are planted, to Succoth in the autumn when they are harvested.

The weekly Sabbath was a time for the dining hall to become less austere. On Friday nights, there were flowers and candles and white linen tablecloths. People came early, and lingered, talking, singing, and dancing horas that made them think of the campfires of Degania.

Democracy and Discipline

The most powerful disciplinary authority in the kibbutz was neither the Secretariat nor some committee appointed for the purpose:

Members of Kibbutz Mayaan Baruch participate in the traditional Sabbath eve celebration. On such occasions, the austere dining hall takes on a festive mood as kibbutzniks sing and dance.

A Kibbutznik Remembers

Love of the land, the work, and the community defined a kibbutznik's life. In Kibbutz Makom, *a pioneer identified only as "Saul" shared his memories of hope and hardship.*

"If you were to ask me whether or not I regret the way of life I have chosen, my clear and sincere answer would be that, were I able to start my life all over again, I would take the same path. I have been here from the time of the first tent and the first tree. This heavy red soil with its basalt rocks was shadowless. During the long hot summer, your own shadow was the only existent shade. Barren land, simple huts and tents, and the joy of creation. The tents were round, conelike; inside were two or three iron beds, and mattresses stuffed with corn leaves which we cultivated in our fields. The closet was a vegetable box, two shelves for our one pair of pants and single shirt— a set of clothes for work and a set for rest. . . . A Van Gogh print decorated the central pole. An oil lamp, a vase, and an Arabian clay jug to hold our water supply were among the meager belongings. . . . In summer, the tent flaps were constantly turned up to allow the wind to blow in and cool our sweating bodies. . . . [W]e used to supplement this cooling system by pouring water on the wooden floor and lying on boards to take a nap."

It was public opinion. In a society that placed such importance on the group, "What will people think?" was a vitally important question, which operated as a reliable social control in many situations.

Melford Spiro offered a telling example of the power of opinion in *Kibbutz: Venture in Utopia*:

[The kibbutz] celebrates the festival of Passover with an annual public *Seder*, or Passover ceremony, to which friends and relatives outside the kibbutz are invited. Its choir usually plays a prominent part in this celebration, but it had not been diligent in rehearsal attendance this year and there was a strong possibility that it would not be prepared by Passover eve. Three days before the celebration, a notice signed by the Holiday Committee appeared on the bulletin board. The notice stated that only three days remained till Passover, and the choir was not yet prepared because its members had not attended rehearsals. If the choir did not meet the following three nights for rehearsals, the Holiday Committee would recommend . . . that the festival be canceled. Beneath this announcement appeared the names of the choir members, and the sections in which they sang. The notice had its desired effect. Rehearsals were held with full attendance each night, and the choir sang at the *Seder*.[28]

If public opinion failed to correct a problem, more formal procedures were available. Someone could bring a member's offense to the attention of the whole kibbutz, through discussion in the general assembly. Often, just the threat of being criticized in front of the whole community was enough to cause the member to rethink his or her position. This is one important effect of a group-centered culture: Even mild forms of discipline get results when the highest value is to belong and to have the respect of one's peers.

Running Out of Options

The grubby, day-to-day realities of living were hard on everyone; the pressures of the group, very real:

> In the kibbutz, a mistake by one person will not only cause him to suffer, but will bring suffering to the entire group. As a result, [the member] is much more careful, as no one wishes to experience the guilt of having caused the group to suffer. One of the chaverim used the wrong chemical when spraying fruit trees. Instead of saving the trees he killed them. When the chaver discovered his mistake, he fell into a deep depression, although no one reprimanded him for a mistake which others could have made just as easily. Nevertheless, although most chaverim were highly sympathetic, he told a chavera that he wanted to kill himself, and in discussing the economic consequences of his error with the secretary, he asked for a rope with which to hang himself.[29]

While such extreme reactions were fortunately rare, kibbutzim—especially new, struggling ones—did have a startlingly high suicide rate. People who were already taxed by the demands of pioneering could be pushed over the edge by some personal tragedy or failure. One founding member of a large and prosperous kibbutz told author Amia Lieblich:

Public opinion was the most powerful disciplinary authority on the kibbutz. Workers were often driven to excel at their tasks for fear of public criticism if they made a mistake.

While life on the kibbutz was never easy, many kibbutzniks took great pride in their communities and the kibbutz movement.

had drastically changed our life-style from that of middle-class intellectuals to that of homeless day laborers, often hungry and sick with fever. . . . It was a profound inner struggle. Work was the highest value in life, yet work was terribly difficult physically, especially in this heat. In the kibbutz, a person was judged by his working ability, and some of the people who were used to being popular and respected in their former environments were suddenly despised and scorned here, since they couldn't stand the difficult work. There was a great amount of friction. It's much more demanding to live constantly among friends than to meet them periodically. . . . All this proved to be too demanding for some, and they simply couldn't cope with the situation.[30]

Even for those who could cope, kibbutz life was not easy. Many joined a community only to leave when they could not adjust to the punishing workload, the primitive living conditions, the lack of privacy and individual freedom. The dropout rate was high. Faithful kibbutzniks soon decided that the future of their movement lay in education. They would raise whole generations of children who would accept communal living as completely natural, who would see no reason to doubt or debate its superiority. In this way, the founders hoped to build communities that would grow naturally from within, becoming the vanguard of a new and better Yishuv.

Some people couldn't take this kind of life. . . . We had many suicides in the beginning. . . . Two or three of them nearly destroyed the community. . . . It's difficult to understand the reasons for that kind of desperation. It was a very young society; the majority of the people were eighteen or nineteen years old; the "elders" were in their twenties. All of us

3 Children of the Dream

Growing up on the kibbutz was a unique experience, shaped and defined by the fact that kibbutz youngsters lived apart from their parents in a special "children's house." Over the years, child development experts have studied this system, seeking to understand how communal upbringing affected the lives of parents, children, and the kibbutz community as a whole.

Children were grouped together by age and cared for by a woman called a *metapelet* (plural *metaplot*), who was specially trained for her job. From infancy to adolescence, children slept in their own dormitories, ate in their own dining hall. Though most of them visited their parents every day, the children's house was their true home.

The Nursery

In most kibbutzim, a baby remained with its mother for the first six to eight weeks of life. During that time, the mother did not have to worry about her normal duties in the kibbutz. She was free to devote all her time to the baby.

After newborns reached six to eight weeks of age, they entered the communal nursery or "infants' house" and the *metapelet* took over routine care. Though most kibbutzim did not allow parents to take babies for home visits until they were six months old, both parents could visit anytime they wished. The mother came to the nursery several times a day to feed, dress, and bathe the

From the time they are infants, children live apart from their parents in special communal houses. In these "children's houses," a specially trained metapelet *acts as the primary caregiver.*

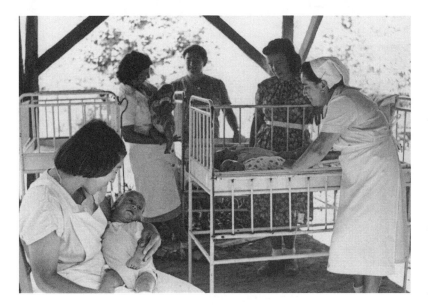

Mothers take time out from their work schedules to visit their children in the infants' house on Kibbutz Givat Brenner.

baby. At night, she tucked him into bed and went back to her own living quarters.

The philosophy behind the children's house was to free the mother from the constant pressure of caring for a new baby, but it was not without its disadvantages, as one young mother told Amia Lieblich:

> During this early period of motherhood, the young mothers are forced into very close contact with each other. It's not enough that they have to adjust to the professional team which takes care of their babies, but they also must become accustomed to the constant company of each other. They sit together in the crowded infants' rooms, breast-feeding their babies, bathing them, whatever. Naturally, there's a lot of friction; a lot of comparison and criticism is going on under the surface, frequently erupting. If you're lucky, you're in pleasant company. [31]

Crawling infants were placed together in large playpens. Barring injury or some other emergency, they were left to their own devices while the *metapelet* took care of housekeeping chores. Bruno Bettelheim described the collective life of these babies in *The Children of the Dream:*

> [T]he children crawl over each other, push each other down, and while at first the pushed down child may wail, he soon learns his place in the pecking order and adjusts accordingly. But life is not just bad times and getting pushed down; most of the time the children play successfully together. Since no parent interferes with the pecking order, and even the metapelet does so only rarely, each child stays in his given place and soon learns to play according to the hierarchy established. [32]

At one of the kibbutzim he studied, Bettelheim interviewed an experienced *metapelet* about the children in her care:

> She told me that there were sixteen in the nursery, but that each metapelet was only responsible for four. "I work four

Once children reach approximately twelve months of age, they move from the nursery to the toddlers' house. These parents feed their children a mid-morning meal at Kibbutz Tuval.

hours in the morning," she said, "from 7:00 to 11:00, and then I return again at 12:30.". . . . I wondered what happens then, between 11:00 and 12:30. . . . The answer was: "They don't need anybody, they're in the playpen during that time."[33]

Toddlers

Between twelve and fifteen months of age, children moved from the nursery to the toddlers' house. There they lived and slept with familiar companions from the nursery group and visited with parents for an hour or two each day. The move still demanded a great deal of adjustment, as Melford Spiro explained:

> [H]e must become adjusted to a new physical environment, at least one new nurse, new (and slightly older) children, a new routine, and new disciplines. In the Toddlers House . . . the infant is gradually toilet trained; he is taught to feed himself; and he learns to get along with his playmates.[34]

This learning process tended to be excessively noisy and somewhat boisterous by nonkibbutz standards. The toddlers had already learned to fend for themselves in nursery playpens. They were not accustomed to adapting to adult routines, or coping with an endless drone of adult commands: "stop jumping around," "behave yourself," "settle down"—and above all, "stop that noise!"

Kibbutzniks gave their toddlers ample opportunity to interact with one another and with their environment. Toddlers' houses were spacious and cheerful, with child-size furniture, cabinets, and countertops. Their playgrounds were often marvels of inventiveness, as Harry Golden observed during his visit to Kibbutz Sa'ad on the edge of the Sinai desert:

> Two [kibbutzniks] had constructed a spaceship, outlined by old piping through the center of which was a slide. A dozen worn tires, set halfway into the ground, formed a tunnel maze. There were the stripped remains of two tractors with refurbished seats on which preschoolers climbed. Supports for the swings and

chinning bar were made from discarded irrigation pipes.[35]

Moving On

At the age of four, children moved to yet another house—the kindergarten, where two or three toddler groups combined into a larger unit of sixteen to eighteen children, who would live together as a unit for the next ten to eleven years of their school careers. They became a *kvutza;* a virtual family to one another, living as brothers and sisters.

Toddlers reacted to the move in a variety of ways. Some had trouble sleeping in their new beds, some missed a favorite toy, or a corner in the play yard they had especially enjoyed. Almost none of them appeared to miss their *metapelet*.

Teachers and *metaplot*, who had seen this behavior many times, talked about it with Dr. Bettelheim:

[T]his year . . . a group moved into the kindergarten house, and on the first day their old metapelet came to dress them in the morning, a boy said, "Why are you here again? I don't want you to be here anymore." This was not just a fleeting reaction, since another metapelet complained: "My old children, when they meet me, don't even greet me. . . . It's me who has to [greet] them till it hurts. And still they don't say anything."[36]

If an American child behaved this way, adults would probably assume that he or she was avoiding the pain of separation by pretending not to care at all. For kibbutz children, this behavior had a different meaning. Even at the tender age of four, they had seen *metaplot* come and go. They had learned that the relationship with any one *metapelet* was never meant to be permanent. Relationships that *were* supposed to be permanent continued undisturbed: Parents still welcomed

Being Strong, Being Free

Kibbutz-born children take equality, strength, and freedom for granted. Because they have never felt like victims, they cannot understand how six million Jews could have perished in the Nazi Holocaust. Peter Hellman captures this attitude perfectly in his introduction to Heroes: Tales from the Israeli Wars.

"A group of kibbutz children stand in silence before a giant enlargement of a famous photograph. They are at the museum of Yad Vashem, Israel's memorial to the Holocaust. . . . The photo, taken in the Warsaw ghetto, shows a boy being marched to an unknown fate by jackbooted, rifle-toting Nazi soldiers. His hands are raised and his thin face is filled with terror.

Although the boy in the photo would have been close to their own age . . . these kibbutz children's faces are blank. Finally, one of them indignantly asks, 'But . . . where was our army?'

Just as the boy in the photo probably could not have imagined a Jewish army existing to protect him, these Israeli children, two generations later, were unable to comprehend that such an army did not then exist to rescue him."

their children's visits, peers still shared their life in a way that no one else had done.

The Kindergarten Years

By the time children reached the kindergarten house, they were so well socialized to the communal environment that they had difficulty functioning away from it. Decision making was especially difficult, as one kibbutz mother explained to Bettelheim:

> Life is much easier here for children, and I speak from experience, because we lived for a couple of years in Paris. . . . At that time my daughter was five, and choosing clothes was an ordeal. The children she went to school with wore varied types of clothing, and though she had quite definite likes and dislikes, she could never make up her mind which of her likes she should choose for herself. Her

In the kindergarten (pictured), toddlers are grouped into units of sixteen to eighteen children. For the next ten to eleven years, the children live together as a virtual family.

indecision in the stores exhausted her and me. But as soon as we came back to the kibbutz, there were no longer any problems for her. She saw everybody dressing the same way. Actually she wanted here and in Paris the same: to conform. But in Paris she never knew what the other children would wear, so she couldn't choose. Here, where everybody wears more or less the same, things were incredibly easy for her.[37]

Though kibbutz children were certainly more group directed than outsiders of the same age, they were also much less dependent upon adults. They could play unsupervised for long periods of time, resolve their own disputes, and schedule their own daily routines. Many parents complained of feeling neglected as children who once relished their daily home visits were suddenly "too busy" to stay for more than a few moments.

At around six years of age, children entered the *kitat maavar* ("transition class"), which included what Americans would call kindergarten and first grade. There they learned the fundamentals of reading, writing, and arithmetic, and there they prepared for the next step in their lives.

The Children's Community

At the age of seven, youngsters took their first step into the wider world of the Children's Community, or Children's Society, as it was sometimes called. There they would receive direct, hands-on experience in collective living:

> For the first time children live in a building that includes not only their . . . age-peers, but other children whose ages

As a result of their communal environment, kibbutz-born children tended to have difficulty making decisions on their own and functioning away from the collective.

span a wide range—from seven to twelve. Each . . . group of sixteen children . . . has its own teacher, classroom, and bedroom. But the entire student body eats together, plays together, and participates in the same extracurricular activities. Hence, the functional "children's society" for these children includes not only their [group], but the entire school population.[38]

In this community-within-a-community, the children operated a garden where they got hands-on training in agriculture while growing a sizable portion of their own food. They planned, planted, maintained, and harvested the crops. They also scheduled their own work periods, cleaned their own quarters, and held their own general assemblies to discuss issues facing the group and to deal with interpersonal conflicts. Adults were

In the Children's Community, youngsters received hands-on training in communal living. They operated their own community garden and cared for livestock and poultry.

Children of the Dream   **39**

available to help if needed, but the children rarely had to ask.

It was a busy life—sometimes too busy, according to some kibbutzniks who grew up in Children's Communities. One young woman recalled her experiences for Amia Lieblich:

Now that I compare the life of adults here to the children's life, I think that kids live under more pressure than adults. . . . Children study, work, and must also be very active socially. Children work seriously here, doing a great part of the mass seasonal farming work. They also work very hard preparing cultural events. Every season has its holiday or central event for which the children's society must prepare. In the summer it's camps, in the spring it's field trips—an endless chain of social events, each one prepared to perfection. You can never relax. And, of course, there's homework and visits with your family; you never have a moment for yourself. When you are finally in your room, it's shared with two other kids and it's never quiet. It's very crowded in the children's dorms; that's why every kibbutz child dreams of the private room he gets upon returning from the Army.[39]

School Days, Kibbutz Style

Classroom atmosphere in the kibbutz was as direct and egalitarian as every other aspect of kibbutz life. Children called teachers by their first names, and helped to shape their own curriculum. There were no tests, no grades, no threats of being held back for failing to perform up to a prearranged standard.

Dan Leon found that the kibbutz school "is based upon respect for the individual personality and potential of each child, and upon mutual trust between pupil and teacher, rather than blind and impersonal discipline. It strives above all to nurture the . . . poten-

---

Kibbutz Education: Flaws and Failings

Though kibbutz education was well suited to the task of preparing students for collective living, it was not without flaw, as author Amia Lieblich discovered in her interviews with teachers and metaplot, *published in her book* Kibbutz Makom.

"[Kibbutz] educators . . . often describe their students as spoiled, unwilling to exert themselves in their study or work, and lacking initiative. Adults who belong to the second generation . . . frequently cited mediocrity as the general product of the communal education system. In their view, this is the result of a permissive education which does not make any challenging demands, thus extinguishing personal ambition and inhibiting the individual desire to excel. Children learn that conformity and loyalty to the norms of the group are the preferred values; they become primarily concerned with criticism from their peers. . . . There is certainly a quest on the part of parents and educators alike for a solution that would combine the benefits of a collective school and a conservative family life with the advantages of the innovative educational system created by the kibbutz."

tial of the student so that he can think and work things out for himself."[40]

Kibbutz children were unaccustomed to rules handed down by parents, teachers, or other authority figures. Their rules grew naturally, out of the need to function as part of the peer group. Even the youngest among them worked in the garden and studied in the classroom because doing such things was their social duty, and because the whole group would suffer if one person failed in this duty.

Group pressure was not the only reason that young kibbutzniks kept up with their studies. Kibbutz educators went to some lengths to devise interesting programs. Instead of self-contained classes that had no relationship to one another, students learned by the project method. Built around a central theme, the project method incorporated a variety of interdisciplinary learning activities.

In a unit on transportation, for example, the children would study the development of transportation in history class; write about it in Hebrew composition; study the principles of motion, speed, and distance in science; draw different vehicles in art; and perhaps learn to read maps, figure mileage, and estimate fuel costs in math. At the end of the project, they would arrange a display and demonstration of their work, inviting parents to a special program.

Growing Up Jewish

Jewish history and tradition were a large part of the curriculum. Even the most secular kibbutzim used the Bible as a fundamental text on history, as well as teaching Jewish ethical, moral, and social values. Like the first kibbutzniks at Degania, later kibbutzniks considered it important for their children to

During an "Ancient Ways Workshop," children learn about their Jewish heritage. This kibbutznik demonstrates the ancient way of making olive oil.

learn of their Jewish heritage, as Dan Leon explained:

The children's participation in their celebration expresses their own roots in the soil as they bring in the first-fruits of their own farm, plant a tree on Tu'beshvat [Jewish arbor day], or build their own Succoth [autumn harvest booth]. Chanukah, with its unforgettable ceremony of the kindling of the lights, and [Passover], which is one of the highlights of the whole kibbutz year, recall episodes of Jewish heroism in the long struggle for liberation. . . . The children look forward to the festivals eagerly, for each one has a special excitement of its own.[41]

In Jewish religious tradition, bar/bat mitzvah (literally, "son/daughter of duty") is a rite of passage for thirteen-year-olds. It marks the "age of accountability" when a young person formally becomes responsible for his or her own deeds and assumes the religious duties of an adult. The candidate studies for weeks, learning to chant a portion of the Hebrew Scriptures. On the appointed day, he or she recites the portion before an assembled congregation, then gives a brief talk, usually affirming commitment to Jewish values. The occasion ends with family and friends' showering the young person with gifts and welcoming him or her as a full participant in Jewish life.

In kibbutzim, the ceremony took on a whole new character. The young person assumed cultural duties rather than religious ones, and the preparation went far beyond learning to read a portion of Scripture in biblical Hebrew.

In those settlements where enemy attack was an ever-present threat, bar mitzvah and bat mitzvah candidates had to show that they were ready to help defend their homes. Many kibbutzim were close to unfriendly neighbors, or so isolated that they were vulnerable to raids by sporadic bands. Each candidate took his or her turn walking a guard post, and had to demonstrate a knowledge of survival skills by spending a night at a "wilderness camp" some distance from the kibbutz. A kibbutz bar/bat mitzvah was designed to show that the candidate was ready to assume the responsibilities of citizenship, as a youth worker explained to Michael Gorkin:

> "Traditionally . . . bar mitzvah has been a religious celebration. . . . Yet what meaning can a religious celebration have for kibbutz children? . . . That's the question

our fathers had to ask themselves. And what they decided is that bar mitzvah still applies. Instead of religious duties, there are other duties—to the kibbutz, for instance. Or to the country. And also, since we are a society where men and women count equally, boys *and* girls celebrate together."

Much of the celebration is symbolic. . . . For a month or so prior to the bar mitzvah date, the boys and girls performed tasks—thirteen altogether—which symbolized their coming of age. Some of these tasks were simple; working a full day instead of the usual two hours per week; or writing a letter to a member of [Parliament] . . . and receiving a response. But other tasks were more unfamiliar: for example, using money to take a bus into town—Tel Aviv or Haifa—and spending a night alone with some family. "All of this may seem a little silly and unimportant . . . but to us, to the children involved, it's a big moment." [42]

The Wider World of High School

A kibbutz high school generally covered what in the United States would be grades seven through twelve. Only the largest kibbutzim maintained their own schools. Most combined with one or more other settlements to form a larger, regional school. There students basically formed a little kibbutz, as they once had constituted a Children's Community.

The young people set up a student government based on the structure of their home kibbutzim, with committees elected by the student body to be responsible for work schedules, social affairs, and cultural life. The

While high school students were instructed in some agricultural subjects, they received a liberal education that emphasized the humanities.

students thus received hands-on training in the principles of collective government, so they would be prepared for the time when they assumed their places as full members of the kibbutz.

Those who expected schools run by farming settlements to teach nothing beyond agriculture, home economics, and tractor repair were in for a major surprise. The curriculum, according to Melford Spiro,

> is more nearly like that of the European *gymnasium* than of the American public high school. Although the students will eventually become farmers and workers, there are relatively few "technical" subjects, and no "home economics." The emphasis is rather on a broad liberal education, with special emphasis on the humanities—particularly history, literature, and the arts—including music and painting.[43]

Extracurricular activities reinforced classwork in every field of interest. The musically talented student could join the choir, band, or orchestra. There were drama clubs,

sports teams, and art clubs, as well as school newspapers and literary societies for those interested in writing. With so much to do, these extracurricular groups tended to serve a double purpose. Rehearsals and meetings were often treated as social occasions, providing a chance for members to have a good time sharing an activity that they all enjoyed.

Pairing Off

In general, the social life of teenage kibbutzniks was very different from that of American high school students. Spiro explained the kibbutznik attitude:

> "Dating," in the sense of taking a girl to a dance, a movie, a party, etc., does not exist. Social dancing, indeed, is not found in any form, although folk-dancing is a favorite activity. Related to this non-dating pattern is the absence of make-up on the part of both girls and boys. The typical dress for either sex for any occasion . . . consists of shorts and blouse. In colder weather girls wear skirts, and boys wear khaki trousers.[44]

Children of the Dream

The absence of dating did not mean that kibbutz teenagers never paired off into couples, but they tended to do so later than American teens. This was not "going steady," as Americans understand the term, nor did it necessarily end in marriage or even long-term commitment. To a kibbutznik, being "popular" in the sense of having many boyfriends or girlfriends was a mark of promiscuity. The first unwritten rule of pairing off was "one partner at a time."

The second unwritten rule was "never get involved with a member of your own *kvutza*." To kibbutzniks, becoming romantically involved with someone from your own house would be like going with a brother or sister: taboo. Teenagers did develop boyfriend-girlfriend relationships with members of their own kibbutz, but the partner always came from a different *kvutza*.

Living Legends

In individualistic cultures, adolescent rebellion is part of a young person's struggle toward independence. It is accepted as a fact of life. In the kibbutz, things were very different.

There, people of all ages shared a similar worldview and standards of behavior. More importantly, to rebel against their parents, teenagers would have to attack their own most admired models. Their parents were true pioneers: sturdy, courageous men and women who escaped the ghettos to build a home in the land of their forebears. Their offspring could never duplicate that achievement. Bruno Bettelheim explained the dilemma:

These adolescents cannot throw off parental inhibitions, because it is not true for them as it was for their parents that their elders seemed puny figures, willing slaves of the ghetto. To them, their parents seemed true giants. The inhibitions imposed by ghetto parents were part of what had preserved a semislavery; good reason to throw them overboard. To the kibbutz-born generation, their parents loom as the great figures who brought freedom to the Jews in the face of a whole

Extracurricular activities allowed high school students to explore fields of interest, while also providing a chance for members to socialize.

Rather than turning out rugged individualists, the educational system of the kibbutz produced people who defined themselves in terms of the collective.

doubting world. . . . The first generation found its glory in successfully overthrowing the world of their parents, as they tell their children again and again. But now youth is asked to find equal satisfaction by doing just the reverse. They are expected to rejoice that no more glories are left for them to win, because their parents have reaped them, every one.[45]

The Conscience of the *Kvutza*

Just as being the offspring of living legends had its difficulties, so did belonging to a close-knit *kvutza*. As Bettelheim explained:

With very rare exceptions they cannot buck the group, not for a moment; it is too threatening. This is where their emotional security resides. Without the peer group they are lost. Fifteen or sixteen years of living not as an individual but as an integral part of a peer group has made it nearly impossible for them to conceive of standing up alone against the group. Not only have they been taught this is unpardonable, but they have no experience whatsoever that a single person could go it alone.[46]

By American standards, this sacrifice of individuality would be intolerable. By kibbutz standards, it made perfect sense. A collective society needed people who defined themselves in terms of the group, who lived communally because it was natural for them to live that way. Any educational system that produced such people would not turn out many rugged individualists; this was a fact that the kibbutzniks acknowledged and accepted. To them it was a worthwhile trade-off, made to ensure the survival of a way of life they had come to love.

The Kibbutz and Its Arab Neighbors

For years, Kibbutz Ashdot Ya'acov was a frontier outpost on the Jordanian border. The kibbutzniks worked their land, guarded their borders, and lived with the knowledge that they were the first line of defense against an implacably hostile neighbor. The state of siege ended on October 26, 1994, when Israel and Jordan signed a treaty that ended nearly fifty years of hostilities.

By February of 1995, the people of Ashdot Ya'acov were planning to build a tourist resort at the border they once patrolled with machine guns. They had selected a location perfect for such a resort—a picturesque island surrounded by the waters of the Jordan and Yarmuk Rivers. The kibbutzniks have high hopes for their island getaway. They expect it to attract people from all over Israel, as well as Jordanians who will cross the open border for a night of entertainment with their neighbors on the kibbutz.

Two Peoples, One Land

Friendship still feels awkward to people on both sides of this ancient conflict. The hatred and distrust have lasted a very long time, so

Once the first line of defense against its marauding Arab neighbors, Kibbutz Ashdot Ya'acov (pictured) now plans to transform the frontier outpost into a tourist resort.

The Many Faces of Prejudice

The hostility between Arabs and Jews has sometimes taken a turn that forces people to confront their own prejudices. For kibbutzniks, who generally pride themselves on being reasonable and fair-minded, even small confrontations can be painful. One such incident, related in Sleeping on a Wire, *occurred when an Arab physician took his children to a public swimming pool on a kibbutz near his home.*

"[T]he woman selling the tickets suddenly heard the children speaking Arabic and said, Just a minute. Wait outside. I have to find something out. Then she comes back and says, I'm sorry, this is a private pool. . . . I took the woman to one side, and I told her that what really irked me was that I didn't know how to explain it to my kids on the way home. You tell me what to say them. . . . I hope that because of this refusal my children and your children will not meet on two sides of a rifle fifteen years from now. . . . [The woman] burst out crying. Afterward it turned out that she is a Holocaust survivor, and maybe she saw herself in a situation that seemed like somewhere else. I don't know. We went home. They called later from the pool and apologized, and invited us to come again, for free, but we didn't go."

---

long that hardly anyone remembers how it all began. Beneath the expert analysis and complex theories, one fact seems clear: The animosity between kibbutzniks and Arabs is bound up with their mutual love for the land.

Prior to the formation of the State of Israel, Palestinian Arabs had lived on the land for generations, but they did not own it. Title rested with wealthy absentee owners, who were within their rights to sell it without consulting the tenants. Thus, land title passed to Zionist groups that had collected donations from all over the world to buy it. In some cases, the Arab tenant farmers knew nothing of the transaction until someone came to evict them from their homes.

The kibbutzniks took possession under legitimate agreements with the new legal owners. By all the laws they knew, they had a right to be there. They settled down to the business of building communities that would become the backbone of a reborn nation.

In keeping with their Zionist ideals, they used Jewish labor whenever and wherever possible. This policy threw Arab laborers out of work at a time when many of them were still trying to cope with the loss of their homes, contributing to rising tensions between the two groups.

Showdown at Degania

The insistence on Jewish labor began with the Deganians. Not only did they refuse to hire non-Jewish workers, they insisted that the contractor building their permanent settlement do the same, inserting a clause in the contract specifying that Jewish labor be used wherever and whenever possible. When the Deganians became convinced that the builder was not making a good-faith effort to find qualified Jewish craftsmen, their response was swift and pointed. They vowed to tear down the whole village if it was built by non-Jewish hands. Everyone connected with the project was taken aback—the contractor; the World Zionist Organization, which provided the construction funds; and the Arab workers who would lose their jobs.

The kibbutzniks would not budge, as Joseph Baratz explained:

> For appearances sake [the contractor] brings a Jewish building worker from Safad . . . and also Jewish stone masons from Jerusalem. All the rest are Arabs and these also prepare the foundations. . . . [T]here are not many Jewish building workers and stone masons. But there are some and we accepted the fact that this will prolong the construction. Shall we betray our principles merely because costs would be increased?[47]

The answer was no. The kibbutzniks' insistence on Jewish labor was a major reason that the project took two full years. Despite the fact that the delay forced them to remain in Um Juni longer than they would have preferred, they endured the hardships and unsanitary conditions without complaint. To them, the wait was entirely worthwhile.

The Arabs who lost their jobs saw things differently. The tension between the two groups did not erupt into warfare, but it did result in mutual hostility. According to Mark Tessler, "Degania was isolated and sometimes dangerous. It was necessary to patrol the fields of the settlement, and sometimes to drive away local Arabs who tried to harvest its crops. There were also occasional skirmishes with Arab bands."[48]

Kibbutz and Village

Degania's problems were echoed at other kibbutzim as the movement grew and prospered. Arab neighbors became increasingly uneasy as some were displaced from their land and others were thrown out of work because the kibbutzim refused to hire non-Jews. The gulf between the two cultures widened.

Well-meaning people on both sides continued to hope for peaceful coexistence. Those who wanted a reason to be optimistic could point to the many individual friendships the Jews and Arabs developed in their rural communities. Mark Tessler speaks of "the cordiality that often characterized interpersonal relations between Arabs and Jews in Palestine. . . . [I]t was common for Arabs and Jews in rural communities to visit one another, attending weddings, circumcisions, and so forth in each other's villages."[49]

As time passed, such hopeful signs of peace and friendship became increasingly rare. Arabs saw kibbutzniks as invaders who

As skirmishes increased between kibbutzniks and Arab bands, kibbutzniks were forced to maintain guard posts to prevent attacks on their communities.

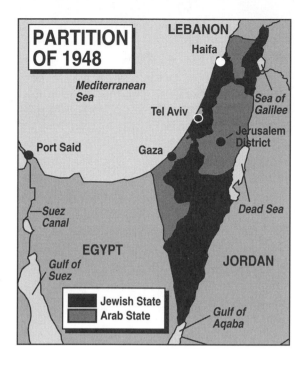

PARTITION OF 1948

LEBANON

Haifa

Mediterranean Sea

Tel Aviv

Sea of Galilee

Jerusalem District

Port Said

Gaza

Suez Canal

Dead Sea

EGYPT

Gulf of Suez

JORDAN

■ Jewish State
□ Arab State

Gulf of Aqaba

had snatched away their beloved land. Kibbutzniks saw Arabs as rivals for the thing they valued most of all: the land they loved and tended and claimed as their rightful heritage.

When the United Nations partitioned Palestine in 1948, creating the State of Israel, thousands of Arabs abandoned their homes and fled or were expelled to make way for Jewish settlement. Others stayed to become citizens of Israel, placing themselves under a Jewish government rather than leave their homes. But many of those who stayed lost their lands anyway, as Israeli journalist Danny Rubinstein reported in his book *The People of Nowhere:*

> [The Arabs of Israel] were bewildered by what had befallen them. After all, they had done all the right things. They had stayed put in their villages and become citizens of the state. Why, then, should they be deprived of their property? "Although many inhabitants of our village

fled," wrote Arabs from the Galilee in a letter published in the government-sponsored Arabic daily *al-Yom* ("The Day") . . . "we decided to remain under [the government] of an honest and democratic state that advocates freedom and equality. But then suddenly members of the neighboring kibbutz came and seized our fertile coastal lands."[50]

Other Arab citizens offered similar complaints, as representatives of several Galilean villages stated in a 1963 press conference:

> As people who love the land . . . we have remained here . . . and we hope to be treated amicably by the authorities. [But] we have discovered that the opposite is the case. . . . The [confiscation] of [1,250 acres] of our agricultural land . . . is a blow that strikes at the very essence of our being.[51]

The Meaning of Exile

In the aftermath of such traumatizing events, kibbutzniks and Arabs abandoned any semblance of cooperation and friendship. They became implacable enemies who could not risk seeing one another as human beings. In spite of this stereotyping, however, flashes of human understanding did sometimes appear. One of the most eloquent descriptions of the Arab exile was written by a kibbutznik, Shmaryahu Gutman of Kibbutz Na'an, who took part in the mass expulsion of Arabs from the towns of Ramle and Lydda. His powerful description of that event was published under a pen name in *Mibifnim* (*From Within*), a publication of the United Kibbutz Movement:

A young Arab refugee clutches a jar of milk while walking through a camp for displaced Palestinian Arabs.

Masses of people marched one behind the next. Women bore bundles and sacks on their heads; mothers dragged children after them. Old and young, women and children marched. Many were young men who could have been fighting in the army; they, too, went into exile. Loaded carts were drawn by animals; hundreds of carts, dozens of carts being drawn not by donkeys but by people. There wasn't a single person who wasn't weighed down by some burden. Even every child carried something: a basket of food, a jug of water, a coffeepot. . . . Through binoculars I saw the masses of people marching toward the village of Barfilya . . . swirls of dust rising in their wake. From close up it was sad to watch this trek of thousands going into exile. As soon as they left the city, they began to divest themselves of things . . . and the roads were cluttered with the belongings that people had abandoned to make their walk easier. . . . They also led goats, sheep, cows, even chickens.[52]

Kibbutzniks knew a great deal about exile. Their ancestors had been exiled from more places than anyone cared to remember. They themselves had left familiar surroundings to build new lives. The Palestinians, they believed, could do the same. Danny Rubinstein summed up this point of view:

After all, the Palestinians [exiled from Israel and now] living in Jordan, Lebanon, Syria, and the West Bank and Gaza Strip (up until 1967) were not subject to foreign rule. They lived under sovereign Arab governments, pursued an Arab way of life, spoke their own language, and practiced their religion. Why, then, should they be bitter?[53]

Most kibbutzniks could not understand why the Arabs would want to stay in a country where they had no territorial sovereignty. To the Jewish pioneers, tending the land was not a goal in itself, but a means to the end of building a new society. Every row they furrowed, every seed they planted, was another small victory in the long struggle for national identity.

Arabs loved the land for its own sake. Their unwavering devotion to a specific house or plot of land mystified the kibbutzniks. It was a powerful bond that went beyond logic or politics, linking the person's sense of self to the place he called home, as Danny Rubinstein explained:

The Israeli reading of the situation dictates political behavior that is radically different from that of the Palestinian Arabs. It was no coincidence that during the withdrawal from the Rafah salient in 1982 (consummating the peace arrangements between Israel and Egypt), it never occurred to any Israeli Jew to continue living in the district that was being turned over to Arab rule. . . . One can even be so bold as to [guess] that Israelis will not live in this country at all unless it remains a Jewish state. Otherwise they would feel as if they were living in exile. . . . On the other hand, Arabs whose homes fall within the [boundaries] of . . . Israel will continue living in them, [because] life in an independent Palestinian state [without] their homes and land would be exile for them.[54]

Battle of the Borderlands

Displaced Palestinians were not the only ones who opposed the kibbutzim. The Arab nations surrounding Israel posed a constant threat to settlements near their borders. Not only did these kibbutzniks have to defend themselves from possible attack, they served as the first line of defense for the country as a whole. For many years civil defense procedures were an integral part of life on a border kibbutz. Kibbutzniks learned to handle rifles just as they learned to handle farm equipment. Guard duty was a normal part of the workday, for the border could never be left unpatrolled.

Even the youngest children learned the meaning of the alarm that signaled imminent attack. They would stop what they were doing and proceed in an orderly fashion to underground shelters, where they would wait out the bombing. At Kibbutz Bilat near the Jordanian border, nightly shellings became so routine that the children slept in the bunkers.

When Michael Gorkin asked a kibbutznik if the younger children were frightened when

After being exiled from the newly partitioned State of Israel, Palestinian Arabs took refuge in crowded camps.

bombs fell, he was stunned by the answer he received. The children accepted the situation quite matter-of-factly, he was told. The shelters were strong enough to withstand even a direct air attack. The children knew this, so why should they be afraid?

The most immediate problem, she continued, was that the shelters were ugly and sometimes uncomfortable. But this, too, was being taken care of. All ten of the children's shelters were now equipped with air-conditioners, and in most of them, something was being done to brighten up the walls. In the younger children's houses, they were using drawings made by the children themselves, and everyone seemed to like them. But even with these improvements, the shelters looked like wine-cellars, and with the double-decker beds (used to conserve space), it was impossible to make them look *very* beautiful. She thought the solution was to do what they had done with the two newest shelters: to use a large square room with single beds along the floor. This way it wouldn't look like a shelter.[55]

The kibbutznik assured Gorkin that these cosmetic measures kept the children happy. Her own eight-year-old slept in the shelter every night, she said, and was perfectly content. An adult always went down when bombs started to fall.

She managed to make the whole thing sound very normal, as if the children were never frightened, the parents never concerned: "Some [parents] are [concerned]," she admitted. "Not many, a few. The point is that we're not all running around like a bunch of chickens with our heads chopped off. We're rather calm about it, as a matter of

fact. Maybe to *you* this doesn't seem possible, but that's the way it is."[56]

The Kibbutz Goes to War

Kibbutzniks cultivated this matter-of-fact, hardened attitude in order to live with the violence that had touched their lives more often than they wanted to remember. Theirs was a world that demanded constant vigilance. Learning to handle a rifle and walk a guard post was part of being a kibbutznik, as a former kibbutz security officer explained:

We trained all our members in the use of weapons. . . . We had around-the-clock

The children of Kibbutz Tel Katyir are cared for in the safety of their underground bomb shelter while Syrians attack their commune.

guard duty, and all the adults took turns, women as well as men. During periods of tension, we had six to eight people on duty every night. Usually there were a pair of guards in each station, one awake and another sleeping, just in case.[57]

The group mentality of the kibbutz and the skills acquired in defending their communities made kibbutzniks excellent soldiers. They willingly took on the most dangerous missions and never backed down from a battle or deserted a comrade in time of danger. The people of Israel hailed them as heroes, but kibbutznik soldiers saw more irony than heroism in their military exploits: "[N]o single group in Israel has been so systematically brought up in a spirit of humanitarian idealism as these young products of kibbutz society," wrote journalist Amos Elon in his book *The Israelis: Founders and Sons.* "[A]t the same time, no group in the Israeli population has a better fighting record."[58]

Statements of young kibbutzniks who fought in the Six-Day War of 1967, between Israel and an Arab alliance led by Egypt, showed a strong sense of duty and a determined lack of hatred for the Arabs who had been their enemy: "None of the participants . . . doubted the justice of their cause; they saw it not in terms of ideology but of survival. None rejoiced in victory. Few could forget the scenes of suffering, or overlook the price paid by both victors and vanquished." One young man said that his most vivid memory of the war was his own relief when he fired at an Egyptian soldier and missed. "I had to shoot," he said, "but I was glad that he got away." Another remembered a more terrible event:

There it was, the tank, that a short time ago had attacked us. It was hit . . . going

All members of the kibbutz were trained to handle a rifle and maintain a guard post. Here, an elderly kibbutznik takes his turn at guard duty.

up in flames . . . a figure emerged from it . . . all in flames moving towards an Israeli jeep in dazed agony . . . a moving torch all ablaze . . . the men in the jeep killed him . . . he may have died anyway . . . his death was inevitable. But not to those who shot him. During the day, when they go about their work, they may forget him . . . but at night he will be there all right. He'll be there with them when they dream and when they wake.[59]

"The Children Will Grow Up to Be Soldiers"

Wartime killing is not the only horror that haunts the dreams of kibbutzniks. Terrorist raids, swift and vicious, challenged the kibbutzniks' courage and will to survive. On

April 7, 1980, five terrorists slipped across the Lebanese-Israeli border into Kibbutz Misgav Am and occupied the toddlers' house, holding six children and a young kibbutz father as hostages. The siege began at midnight and ended at 10:30 A.M., when a crack antiterrorist unit of the Israeli army stormed the dormitory. When the fighting ended, all five Palestinians, two Israelis, and a two-and-a-half-year-old boy lay dead.

David K. Shipler described the scene, as he observed it after the gun battle:

> Wind blew through the shattered windows of the nursery, whipping shredded, brightly colored curtains like torn battle flags. The walls behind the cribs were peppered with pockmarks. . . . Toys on shelves stood cracked and splintered by bullets. Spent brass cartridges from the terrorists' . . . rifles lay scattered on the floor, among tiny shoes and toy teacups and books of fairy tales.[60]

Three days later on the Israeli-occupied West Bank, Shipler interviewed a group of young Arab women, who thought the terrorists were justified in their actions. "Even when they threaten and kill children?" asked Shipler.

> "The children will grow up to be soldiers," [one girl] explained. "It's the way to get our land."

> "They don't care if they kill *our* children," said [another girl]. She smiled, and everyone broke into giggles.

At about the time of Shipler's interview, Israeli troops were breaking up an anti-Israeli demonstration at a nearby men's college.

> "We are going to do to you what they did at Misgav Am," [the students shouted].

Efforts Toward Peace

Kibbutzniks have taken an active role in many programs to encourage peace between Arabs and Jews. These are not high-level, government-to-government negotiations, but attempts to bring ordinary people together in friendship. David K. Shipler discusses such programs in Arab and Jew: Wounded Spirits in a Promised Land.

"In the Galilee, Interns for Peace took Jews and Arabs in their twenties and had them live for two-year tours in Arab villages and Jewish towns, where they organized visits between Arab and Jewish schools, sports field days . . . and other activities to bring Arabs and Jews into personal contact. In Nazareth, a group placed Arabs in volunteer work on kibbutzim during the war in Lebanon. . . . At Givat Haviva, in the Galilee, the Hashomer Hatzair kibbutz movement of the Mapam socialist party maintained an institute for Arab-Jewish studies to sensitize teachers and others to issues in promoting tolerance between the peoples."

Then soldiers swarmed through the gate and over the walls, firing tear gas into the rooms, breaking down doors, and beating and hauling students to jeeps and paddy wagons. . . . Forty-one students were injured, six seriously enough to be hospitalized.[61]

To the Israeli soldiers who stormed the campus that day, there was more at stake than ending a civil disturbance. They were taking some measure of revenge for the children of Kibbutz Misgav Am.

The Face of the Enemy

With such hatred on both sides, the prospects for peace seemed dim. Even in times of relative calm, kibbutzniks and Arabs have clung to harsh, one-dimensional stereotypes of each other. Arabs, kibbutzniks claimed, were cowards who shelled helpless civilians and blew up school buses. They were crafty, lazy, and quite unable to appreciate the niceties of civilized living. While kibbutzniks treasured human life, Arabs valued it cheaply.

For their part, Arabs portrayed kibbutzniks as unfeeling fanatics who cared nothing for human rights or human life. Their settlements were armed fortresses where they prepared themselves to kill Arabs and take their land. Even Arabs who did not see kibbutzniks as assault troops plotting an invasion did believe that they were greedy land-grabbers who acquired Palestinian property in highly unethical ways.

An outraged Palestinian from the village of Um Elfahm pled his people's case to David Grossman:

> Look, in Um Elfahm we had 140,000 dunam [35,000 acres] of land before Israel was established, and the Knesset [Israeli parliament] came and made all kinds of laws and confiscated [land] from Israel's Arab citizens. Today two kibbutzim . . . sit on Um Elfahm's land. On our land![62]

As Arabs felt victimized by the loss of the land, kibbutzniks felt threatened by anything or anyone that challenged their right to it. Many believed that peace was impossible until Palestinians gave up their claims to disputed territories and stopped clinging to the memory of their former homes. To break this bond with the past, some kibbutzim razed abandoned Arab villages, planting orchards in their place to obliterate the least sign of anything a homesick exile might recognize as home. The Arabs called this policy heartless and considered it further provocation.

A Collision of Cultures

Land rights may have been the largest issue dividing the kibbutzim and their Arabic neighbors, but it was not the only one. Cultural differences have accounted for much of the difficulty each side faces in communicating with the other. The result has been misinformation, misunderstanding, and all too often, conflict.

For example, the blunt, unadorned speech and straightforward manners of the kibbutznik could be highly insulting to an Arab. The elaborate graciousness of the Arab could seem insincere and fawning to the kibbutznik. Neither side could avoid stereotyping the other, hindering their ability to negotiate from common interests. In spite of deep-seated prejudice, however, the process of learning to see one another as human beings has been going on behind the scenes for many years.

Yaacov Malkin, founder of Beit Ha-Gefen, an Arab-Jewish community center in Haifa, remembers an antipropaganda project that Beit Ha-Gefen organized after the Six-Day War. Captured Syrian and Egyptian officers were invited into Jewish homes for dinner and friendly conversation. One Syrian officer refused to go: He was not interested in a carefully orchestrated evening with a Jewish family. Instead, he wanted to make a tour of inspection, with an Arab driver to take him wherever he wanted to go.

An Israeli Arab who was a member of the center volunteered for the job, and the two spent the day in the lowlands of the Golan Heights:

The captain gave the name of a kibbutz. The driver took him there, and the Syrian stared out the window as they wound slowly through the kibbutz grounds, seeing children at play, families, children's dormitories. The captain asked for a second kibbutz by name, and they went there as well. In all, he had his driver take him to five kibbutzim. . . . [O]n the way back to the [military] prison the Syrian officer sat in silence.

Shortly before reaching the prison, the captain told his driver to pull over and stop. The driver did so, and the captain got out. . . . He walked a short way from the car, off the road, and there he stood

"No Room for Nomads"

The Bedouin tribes have been nomadic herdsmen for hundreds of years, roaming the desert with their flocks and herds. When kibbutzim began to cultivate land in the Negev desert, the Bedouins raided settlements, helped themselves to the crops in the fields, and allowed their goats to graze on kibbutz land. In *Arab and Jew: Wounded Spirits in a Promised Land*, writer David Shipler described the situation as "a clash between antiquity and modernity, a conflict once again between the desert and the settled agrarian life. The Bedouins have wandered the Negev [freely]. . . . [Now] kibbutzim want to irrigate and cultivate. And preservationists want desert zones made into reserves; some argue that the Bedouins are over-grazing and that their black goats damage the fragile desert vegetation. . . . Israeli government policy has evolved on the assumption that the [settled] life represents a positive advancement from the rather unsavory, backward, and undesirable existence of the nomad."

The commander of a special patrol that was formed to keep Bedouins off the kibbutzim and other public lands summed up official policy in one blunt sentence. "If we want a proper country, then there's no room for nomads."

For hundreds of years, Bedouin tribes roamed the Negev desert with their herds.

During a meeting with President Clinton at the White House, Israeli prime minister Yitzhak Rabin (left) enthusiastically shakes hands with Jordan's king Hussein ibn Talal (right).

and wept. Then, after a while, he came back and slipped in beside the driver again. For fifteen years, the captain explained, he had sat in hilltop military positions overlooking those kibbutzim. He had not just thought, he had *known* that they were armed fortresses, pure military bases. . . . Now, he said, he could never tell anybody back in Syria what he had seen here.[63]

Not only would people not believe the Syrian, they would surely think he had been brainwashed.

Moving Towards Peace

On October 26, 1994, King Hussein ibn Talal of Jordan signed a peace treaty with Prime Minister Yitzhak Rabin of Israel. Coming as it did on the heels of formal recognition between Israel and the Palestine Liberation Organization (PLO), the treaty was a harbin-

ger of hope for an area that has known generations of bloody conflict.

On the border, kibbutzim stand down from years of mobilization and former enemies begin to look for new ways to become friends. Once more, as in the 1920s, kibbutzim invite their Arab neighbors to holiday celebrations and return the favor with visits to Arab observances. Young people get together in encounter groups to confront their prejudices. At Givat Haviva in the Galilee, the Hashomer Hatzair kibbutz movement operates an institute for Arab-Jewish studies. And the people of Ashdot Ya'acov are building their island tourist resort on the newly peaceful border.

There is a long way to go. Peace will not replace conflict overnight, and hatred will not disappear simply because two leaders sign a treaty. And while kibbutzniks must come to terms with old religious and racial prejudices, they must also deal with new social and economic challenges that will shape the movement into the next century.

The New Kibbutz: A Community in Transition

Like every living culture the kibbutz has changed with the times. Settlements of rude shacks or battered tents are a thing of the past. Visitors to modern kibbutzim are struck by manicured lawns and meandering walkways; by buildings with simple, clean lines that blend beautifully into the natural environment.

Melford Spiro's description of the kibbutz he called Kiryat Yedidim (to protect the privacy of its members) captured the charm of a well-established and prosperous community:

The kibbutz and the land it works cover an area of approximately 11,000 *dunam* [2,750 acres]. Like the typical European agricultural village, the village proper is situated in a hub . . . from which radiate the various fields and orchards. . . . The houses are laid out in parallel rows on either side of the communal dining hall, which is the physical and social center of the kibbutz. Surrounding the dining room is a large landscaped lawn, which serves to set it apart from other struc-

Kibbutzniks pass by well-tended lawns and lush scenery while taking a leisurely horseback ride through their kibbutz.

tures. . . . The houses themselves are built in the form of ranch-house apartments with, as a rule, four individual living units in each apartment. Each unit consists of one room and, in some cases, a small porch which serves in summer as a second room. Generally, each apartment is separated from the others, as well as from the network of sidewalks traversing the village, by large lawns surrounded by high shrubs. Much attention is devoted to the care of these lawns, and almost every chaver has a flower garden, which he tenderly nurses in the evenings after work.[64]

When Spiro knew it, Kiryat Yedidim was attractive but hardly luxurious. It was a kibbutz of the 1960s, when chaverim still frowned upon materialism or any hint of luxury. By the 1990s, Israeli journalist Z'ev Chafets found a very different atmosphere when he visited Kibbutz Haogen, about an hour's drive north of Tel Aviv on the Plain of Sharon. It had the look and feel of a prosperous rural community. The single room with a sleeping porch that housed one couple had become a three-bedroom apartment that sheltered an entire family group: "[Gary] Hiller, his wife and six children are today's kibbutzniks, [inheritors] of an almost mythical idealism in this small country."[65] A walk from the Hillers' spacious apartment to the dining hall reveals a level of luxury that would have scandalized the founders: "I leave Hiller's . . . apartment and walk across the well-tended lawns toward the dining hall. On the way, I pass a full-sized auditorium, an Olympic-size swimming pool, a modern health and sports facility and a clubhouse."[66]

Back in the days when a handful of sturdy pioneers fought malaria, exhaustion, and bands of hostile raiders, kibbutzniks were cautious about spending their money or changing their ways. Every new idea had to pass the acid test: Was it in the best interest of equality, self-labor, and the ideals of socialism?

"This Will Destroy the Kibbutz"

A founding member of one large community recalled spirited arguments over every detail of operation:

> [I]n those early days . . . we had a formula reaction: "This will destroy the kibbutz." If complete discipline weren't enforced—it would destroy the kibbutz. If we build private bathrooms near the rooms, it would destroy the kibbutz. No, I'm not joking, this was really an argument then. "A private shower will destroy the kibbutz"; I remember its being stated in exactly these words. And later, an electric kettle in the room would destroy the kibbutz, and a radio in the room would certainly do so, too.[67]

Even small variations in routine were perceived as a threat. People became locked into doing everything in a certain way, and any change to set procedure would be greeted with outrage. Sometimes, this dedication to the status quo could become almost comical, as Spiro explains:

> A classic example of [conservatism] involves the scrubbing of the floor in the kitchen in which children's food is prepared. The floor is scrubbed every day, and it is always scrubbed in exactly the same way—starting from a certain wall, and proceeding to the opposite wall. One day, one of the women decided to relieve the monotony by starting at the opposite

On the modern kibbutz, visitors are likely to see spacious apartments (pictured) and manicured lawns, as well as luxurious amenities like swimming pools and health and sports facilities.

wall, although this was less practical. The other women were shocked by this innovation. The floor had *always* been scrubbed starting at the other wall, and that was the *correct* way. Feelings ran so high that one of the women walked out in protest, refusing to work until the floor was scrubbed in the traditional way.[68]

Changing Times

Despite a core-group resistance to anything new and different, the kibbutz did change; in small ways at first, later in ways that shocked more conservative members. The pace of change accelerated as a new generation grew up and began to assume responsibility for governing the kibbutz.

The second generation was born and raised on the kibbutz. For them, the community was not the realization of an ideal, but simply the reality into which they were born. They were more practical and less idealistic than their parents. Rather than worry about philosophy, they wanted a better standard of living, more freedom of choice, and a chance to pursue individual educational and occupational goals.

The sacrifices that had been necessary and even heroic for the first kibbutzniks would have been needless and artificial to their children. To put their personal stamp on the kibbutz, the younger generation had to branch out in new directions. This they did with energy and a great sense of purpose, adding light industry to the economic mix of the kibbutz. But many older members were scandalized at the prospect of bringing factories to the kibbutz. Kibbutzniks were farmers, pure and simple. That was the way it had always been, and that was the way it should remain. To them there could be no higher calling than to work the land, and they had a record of success to support their position.

Not only did kibbutz farming supply the needs of the community, it eventually supplied a good portion of the needs of the nation. According to a 1992 article by journalist Hazael Toledano, "[T]he members of Israeli kibbutzim . . . make up only 3 percent of the Jews in the country (about 130,000). But with their advanced agricultural technology, the kibbutzim produce more than 60 percent of the food consumed by the five million Israelis."[69]

The younger generation agreed that the figures were impressive, but they did not agree that agriculture was the only proper business for the kibbutz. They built factories to make everything from wire cable and plastic containers to socks. Some kibbutzim, like Ma'ale Hahamisha in the Judean hills, opened resort hotels, so city dwellers could spend their vacations in the quiet and clean air of the country.

Industrialization worked, bringing new prosperity to the kibbutz. In time, even the older generation got used to the idea. A factory worker was still a worker, after all, earning a living by the sweat of his brow. Soon, factories and resorts seemed like a natural part of kibbutz culture. Income and profits went up, and for the first time the kibbutzim could spend money to improve their community facilities and raise the standard of living for every member. The lean years were all but forgotten as Israel's kibbutzim went on a spending spree.

Experiments in Private Enterprise

The spree ended with the crash of the Israeli stock market in the mid-1980s, leaving the kibbutzim with their beautiful buildings, their comfortable lifestyles—and a mountain

Many kibbutzim have built factories and resort hotels in attempts to revive their settlements' economy. Guest houses, like this one on Kibbutz Ein Gedi, offer city dwellers the chance to experience the tranquility of the country.

of debt that grew steadily, until it topped $10 billion in 1995. The kibbutzim were suddenly desperate for new sources of income.

Some of the more adventurous members tried their hands at a wide variety of new businesses: day care centers, fast food restaurants, beauty salons, catering services, even law firms. One kibbutz has an advertising agency that bills itself as "the only advertising agency in the world that comes with a cowshed."

When Ze'ev Chafets asked two longtime kibbutzniks how they felt about kibbutzim's renting out their facilities for weddings and engaging in other for-profit enterprises, he received a surprising answer: "'Aside from prostitution, we will do anything to make money these days. We're through being pioneers.' To emphasize the point, she repeats it in English. 'We are not pioneers.'

'But we are still socialists,' adds [another kibbutznik]. 'This is the only place in the world where true socialism is practiced. Only the kibbutz.'"[70]

Less than a year after that interview, Kinneret, second-oldest kibbutz in Israel, committed the most unsocialist act imaginable: It sold shares in its plastics factory on the Tel Aviv Stock Exchange.

It was the first time that an Israeli collective had resorted to such a . . . capitalistic device to raise cash, and the change was a big one. . . . "On the kibbutz, the main thing was always the product," said Shlomo Getz, a member of Kibbutz Gadot in upper Galilee and also a sociologist at Haifa research institute. "Going to the stock market, though, doesn't produce anything—except maybe money. Also, by doing this you clearly separate the industry from the kibbutz itself."[71]

In true socialism, "profit" and "property" are alien ideas. Nothing stands between the worker and his labor, the citizen and his community, the individual and the collective society of

Status of the Worker

Kibbutz respect for the worker is one part of the original philosophy that has withstood the test of time. It comes not only from the communal ideals of socialism, but from the ethical ideas of Judaism. In The Book of Jewish Knowledge, *Nathan Ausubel explains the origins of this attitude.*

"Jewish law . . . went to extraordinary pains to protect the worker, standing alone and quite helpless in ancient society, from exploitation and mistreatment. 'The worker's rights take priority over all other rights,' ruled the Sages of the Talmud. This was as much as laying down the principle that

human rights took precedence over property rights. For that reason, the Jewish law ringed numerous safeguards around the worker's human personality, aside from any considerations about his toil, wages, and other conditions of labor. Many are the references in Jewish . . . literature extolling the spiritual and social importance of work and of the worker. [The prophet] taught in his Wisdom Book, Ecclesiasticus:

But they will maintain the fabric of
    the world,
And in the handiwork of their craft is
    their prayer."

As increasing numbers of people choose to eat in the privacy of their homes, the communal dining hall has become a relic of the past.

which he is a part. Nonetheless, the people of Kinneret are unapologetic about their move into free-market capitalism: "'If we want to compete with the private sector, we need to be able to raise capital,' said Yaron Hermont, Kinneret's secretary, 'and one way to do that is to go into the stock market.'"[72]

Profits from investment, like profits from factory and farm, go into the central treasury for the benefit of the whole kibbutz. In this way, Kinneret pits its communal identity against the inroads of private enterprise. Some members think this balancing act can succeed. Others fear that it will do what hardship and danger were not able to do—destroy the community. In the ongoing debate, both sides agree on one thing: If the kibbutz does survive, it will be changed forever.

The Winds of Change

One of the most far-reaching changes thus far involved that homey, down-to-earth symbol of the pioneering kibbutz: the communal dining hall. In a few short years, it lost its status as

undisputed nerve center of kibbutz life. In most communities, the process began quietly enough, with a few people acquiring hot plates and small refrigerators so they could fix a snack or a cup of tea without walking across the compound. The people who had hot plates and refrigerators liked them; soon, in the natural course of events, everybody wanted hot plates and refrigerators of their own.

At first, few kibbutzniks would have dared to eat an actual meal in their rooms. That would have been an unthinkable breach of protocol. Those who were daring enough to do so anyway went to great lengths to hide their behavior from the chaverim. They smuggled food into their rooms, pulled the shades, locked the door, and only then indulged in this small, forbidden pleasure.

In this unofficial manner, hot plates and refrigerators became normal parts of kibbutz life. No one proposed a resolution or took a vote or debated the issue in open assembly. It just happened. Older members regarded these unplanned, almost unnoticed, changes as especially dangerous. As one pioneer explained, "I would like members to cooperate with the rules and policies, and not to produce slow change by deviating from the rules. There are too many unplanned developments, and we may eventually arrive at a point where we hardly recognize ourselves."[73]

That state of affairs very nearly came to pass with the demise of the dining hall. As living quarters got bigger and more homelike, hot plates and minirefrigerators became fully equipped kitchens. Soon people were eating at home if they happened to be too tired or out of sorts to cope with the noisy dining hall—or simply felt the need for some privacy. After a time, they did not bother to pull the shades so no one would see. In some kibbutzim, members who wanted to "eat in" without having to cook could drop by the communal kitchen for a take-out meal.

In the span of a few years, the communal dining hall went from nerve center of the kibbutz to relic of the pioneering past. Soon only the older generation bothered to eat there regularly. Kitchen workers cut back on the quantity of food they prepared for each meal. By the mid-1990s, some kibbutzim had turned their dining halls into little more than restaurants, with members paying for their meals out of personal allowances given to them by the kibbutz, that in itself a departure from kibbutz practice.

A Matter of Choice

In the beginning, personal budgets were no bigger than an American teenager's allowance. The idea was to allow each member to select personal items like toiletries and clothing without going through the central distribution system. Personal budgets grew as younger kibbutzniks discovered that they liked choosing things for themselves—liked it so much, in fact, that they were not content to limit their choices to aftershave and underwear. By vote of the membership in kibbutz after kibbutz, allowances increased to cover "big-ticket" items such as furniture and household appliances. In time, kibbutzniks all over Israel were buying television sets and motor scooters.

A few adventurous kibbutzim took what they considered to be the next logical step, i.e., tying personal allowance to work performance.

> Since 1991, every member of Neot Mordechai, 30 miles north of the Sea of Galilee, is obliged to work at least 275 days a year; whoever does not meet this requirement has a portion of his personal allowance docked. But these [practical] rules defy the very [principle] of the kibbutz. Although the wages are a relative pittance—no more than $500 a year per working member—their very existence results in the emergence of two classes inside the kibbutz; paid and unpaid workers.[74]

Some members were deeply shocked by this controversial change; others were pleased. Daniel Sziselman, sales manager of a kibbutz sock factory, was one of those favoring economic incentives: "We've lied to ourselves long enough. . . . If the members want a higher income, earnings will have to increase. Ideology is no longer the main motivation of those who live here."[75]

With neither the fierce dedication that inspired the pioneers, nor the lofty idealism that kept them striving against the odds, the new generation of kibbutzniks seems directionless and poorly motivated. Daniel Sziselman and others like him want to fill the gap with personal accountability and objective standards of performance. They aim to create a workplace where individuals are

A laboratory worker tests cosmetics at Kibbutz Mitzpeh Shalem. On some kibbutzim, workers are now paid wages and are held responsible for their performance.

responsible for the quality of their results, and exceptional effort is acknowledged and rewarded.

Lack of accountability has been a problem for some time, according to many long-term kibbutzniks. "You can screw up, ruin a batch of plastic in the factory, and you're not held responsible,"[76] said one American-born kibbutznik. Another man voiced similar concerns to Amia Lieblich: "The only fault I find with our current way of life is the terrible wastefulness I see everywhere. It's a result of the lack of personal responsibility for our expenses. Take electricity, for example; people keep it on for nothing. Or the way they treat cars, as if they don't really belong to them. Or the food waste, and the kind of food people give to dogs here!"[77]

Changes in Child Care and Education

For years, the children's house had been the defining characteristic of the kibbutz movement. Visiting dignitaries wanted to see it,

child development specialists wanted to study it, city-bred Israelis regarded it with a certain awe. Despite this public acclaim, a majority of second-generation kibbutzniks felt that the children's house had served its purpose. It was time to explore other options. One by one, the kibbutzim abandoned their communal lodgings in favor of family-based child care.

Under the family-based sleeping arrangement, the mother becomes the most significant figure, the parents become the main socializers, and the metapelet and the peer group recede in importance. The children's house may be compared to a day care center, the influence of which may be significant in some respects but cannot be compared to the influence of the "classical" children's house.[78]

As ties to the *kvutza* weakened, children were more apt to go their own way, reacting to inner desires rather than outer pressures. In the schools, teachers had to develop new educational methods for individualistic students

On most kibbutzim, family-based child care has become the norm. The children's house, which was once the defining characteristic of the kibbutz movement, is now similar to a day care facility.

no longer motivated to learn by classes without grades, exams, or homework assignments. In one way or another, students had to be held accountable for their work. Some teachers welcomed this opportunity to introduce more structure into the classroom.

One American-born teacher explained the problems she had observed with the leniency that had long been a hallmark of kibbutz schooling:

> The whole atmosphere suppresses any signs of ambition or competition. . . . I firmly believe that we are wrong in our educational approach: Children need a fairly strict framework; they must face challenging demands. Otherwise they grow wild or, at best, become mediocre people. People may tell you there's a great drive to study at a later stage of life, that we have so many university students, etc. I think it is exaggerated. The older generation studies more and more [while] the majority of the young ones, who grew up here, are pretty ignorant and don't even mind.[79]

Ein Zivan: The Kibbutz That Quit

The most startling—and for many, troubling—changes in the kibbutz lifestyle occurred at Kibbutz Ein Zivan in the Golan Heights. In 1993, the general assembly there voted to close down the dining hall and allow its members to "become full-fledged wage earners with no obligation to the community. They can work either in the kibbutz or find a job outside the community. With their earnings they may own private property and pay for the services they get. For all practical purposes, Ein Zivan voluntarily ceased to be a kibbutz."[80]

Ruth Baruch, a member of the Ein Zivan management committee, treated the whole matter with resigned acceptance. People simply would not work hard unless they were paid for it, she said. That was that, and there was nothing more to be said. Ein Zivan fully expected to be drummed out of the United Kibbutz Movement, the 165-community association that was formed with the joining of two pioneer federations, Hakibbutz Hameuchad and Ichud Hakvutzut Vehakibbutzim.

From the standpoint of the United Kibbutz Movement, Ein Zivan is paying too high a price for its economic survival. "'They have tried to make an ideology out of what really is a bad situation,' said Menachem Rosner, a kibbutznik and a sociologist at Haifa University's Institute for Research of the Kibbutz and the Cooperative Idea. 'But Ein Zivan will stand as a symbol of where things may lead. It may have the effect of stopping more far-reaching changes.'"[81]

So far, that has not been the case. In 1995 Kibbutz Beit Oren near Mount Carmel announced that it too would begin paying salaries to its members. Unlike small personal allowances that are the same for everyone, salaries vary in accordance with the value and complexity of the work, just as they do in the United States and other free enterprise systems. Beit Oren's pay scale ranges from $400 a month for an unskilled agricultural worker to $2,500 for a managing executive.

Keeping the Faith

While secular kibbutzim began to lose their ideological focus in this time of transition, the religious Hakibbutz Hadati federation has experienced a resurgence and become an unexpected voice for a return to the pure collectivism of the classical kibbutz. Orthodox religious kibbutzim have existed for decades, surviving on the fringes of a social movement that was avowedly nonreligious. Secular kibbutzim expected them to flounder in the struggle to blend two demanding, and often contradictory, ways of life into a functioning social unit.

Capitalism Versus Socialism

Socialism at its best encourages cooperation; capitalism encourages competition. As the kibbutzim move between the two, there is a cultural impact as well as an economic one. The 1995 Grolier Academic American Encyclopedia *entries on "capitalism" and "socialism" make these fundamental differences clear.*

"Capitalism: 'The marketplace is the center of the capitalist system. It determines what will be produced, who will produce it, and how the rewards of the economic process will be distributed. From a political standpoint, the market system has two distinct advantages. . . . No person or combination of persons can control the marketplace [and] the market system tends to reward efficiency with profits and to punish inefficiency with losses.'

Socialism: 'The term socialism is commonly used to refer both to an ideology . . . and to a state of society based on that ideology. Socialists [claim] to stand [for] equality, social justice, cooperation, progress, and individual freedom and happiness, and they have generally sought to realize these values by the abolition of the private-enterprise economy and its replacement by "public ownership," a system of social control over production and distribution.'"

The most basic contradictions revolved around the Sabbath, strict observance of which is the heart and soul of Orthodox practice. From the first star on Friday evening until sundown on Saturday, nobody works. It is forbidden to kindle a fire, turn on a light, or use knives and scissors. Meals are prepared ahead so that no one has to cook. Many other prohibitions exist, all with one purpose: to set the Sabbath apart from other days, and make it a time of rest and renewal.

On a busy farm, where the cycles of life cannot be measured strictly by calendar and clock, Sabbath-keeping can require great ingenuity, as, for example, at a religious kibbutz called Sa'ad, where members grew roses that were sold to florists all over Israel, and also operated a good-size dairy.

Timing is everything with roses. They must be picked just before blooming. If they are taken from the bush too early, they will not flower at all; too late, and the petals begin to loosen and fall away. The people of Sa'ad resigned themselves to losing 15 percent of their crop every year because of Sabbath blooming.

Some of the more enterprising members were not willing to accept these high losses. They took the problem to the Hebrew University School of Agriculture, where scientists developed a fertilizer that would give plucked roses an extra day of growth. This made it possible for workers to pick immature buds on Friday afternoon, many hours before they were ready to bloom. These cut flowers continued to develop. By Sunday morning, they were ready for sale at the flower markets. The new fertilizer had cut Sabbath losses in half—without compromising Sabbath observance.

Fortunately for the dairymen of Sa'ad, cows are not roses. On Sabbath, the milking is normally done by an automated machine, but if that machine breaks down, the workers may do the milking by hand without fear of violating the Sabbath. In Jewish law, it is forbidden to allow animals to suffer, on the Sabbath as well as any other day.

Milking cows is now done by electrical pumps. These automated machines allow kibbutzniks to observe Sabbath while maintaining their industrial schedules.

Religious versus
Secular Kibbutzim

Though outsiders may find the many laws of Orthodox Judaism confusing, they provide structure and a sense of higher purpose for those who follow them. This structure, in turn, has kept the religious kibbutzim healthy and thriving. Unlike their secular counterparts, they are not so easily swept along with changes in the political or economic climate. Author Yossi Melman quotes Saul Aviel, an officer of the religious kibbutz federation:

So far we don't face the challenge and demand for profound changes as in the rest of the kibbutz movement. Our kibbutzim have not been pressed by their members to privatize themselves. We still have our communal dining rooms and no separation between the production and communal aspects of our life. We have not introduced personal budgets. . . . Because of our religious education and values, we are more solid and less receptive to fashionable changes. I do not know how long it will last. How long can we repel the general atmosphere . . . of hedonism, cynicism and nihilism which threaten the kibbutz movement?[82]

The question is a good one, and no one knows the answer. In the secular federations, socialists who wish to preserve the strict traditions of the kibbutz have formed an organization called Always Kibbutz, which claims four hundred members from throughout the movement. These few people work to preserve their way of life in an increasingly materialistic society. Though they are dedicated and vocal, many of them fear they are fighting a losing battle.

Historian and kibbutznik Henry Near considers this alarmism premature. He points out that the kibbutz has survived for eight decades, a life span that makes it the most successful cooperative community in history. No social movement survives that long without being able to adapt to changing realities. Near foresees a time when the kibbutz will redefine itself: "Ideological straitjackets have been removed, and in 10 or 15 years, you'll have a much greater variety of kibbutzim. . . . But most will be looking for gradual change."[83]

Observers who admire the kibbutz experiment, young people who love their communities, and pioneers who dedicated their lives to those communities are hoping that history will justify Henry Near's faith in the movement and its lifeways.

Community Values, Personal Needs

As the kibbutz moves into the future, perhaps its greatest challenge will be to meet the needs of an increasingly diverse membership. Kibbutz society is more complex than it used to be, with people of different ages, abilities, and interests trying to live together in harmony. Successful communities will be flexible enough to balance the needs of the few with the needs of the many. It will not be an easy task.

The Prickly-Pear Folk

Native-born Israelis tend to be no-nonsense people who waste little time on manners and other niceties. Somewhere along the line, they picked up the nickname sabras, after a barbed but tasty fruit that grows on cacti all over Israel. The name is applied to all Jews born in Israel, but somehow kibbutz sabras seem to have a few more prickles than their city counterparts. Harry Golden explained the image of the sabra in *The Israelis*:

> As a fruit, the sabra is more trouble than it is worth. You cannot buy it in fruit stores nor are you served it in restaurants. Along the roads now and then you see little kids with a tin pail at the end of a long pole trying to dislodge the sabra from the cactus. But as a symbol, the sabra is something else again. There is a sabra generation, a sabra vote, and a sabra [lifestyle]. It is something in Israel to be a sabra.[84]

On the kibbutz, the sabra—brusque, opinionated, and courageous—became a living symbol of that "new and more vigorous Jewish identity" the pioneers had wanted to create. Though the present generation does not spend its days draining swamps and its

Native-born Israelis have been compared to the sabra, a barbed fruit that grows on cacti throughout Israel.

Some kibbutz members worry that the movement has gone too far in trying to free their children from the constraints of polite society.

ners were one of the things we scorned, and now our children don't even use the words "thank you" anymore. We were all the same age, so we forgot manners and respect for the elderly. . . . [W]e have developed an outstanding system of support for old people, but it's not spontaneous. You can see a child standing next to an adult who has dropped something, and the child won't offer his help . . . even for an elderly person. Nobody would offer his seat to an older person in a bus. It's as if we have stretched the sense of equality to an absurd degree.[85]

The sabras themselves echo this concern about the kind of people they have become, and the kind of people their children are becoming. As members of the *kvutza*, they can be secure and apparently self-sufficient. As individuals, they are often passive and unwilling to exert themselves to personal achievement. According to Amia Lieblich's informant, this comes from growing up in a culture that

nights dancing horas, kibbutzniks are still a people apart, different somehow from mainstream society. Not all of their differences are positive. Like people everywhere, kibbutz sabras have their faults as well as their virtues.

Their pride can turn to arrogance, their determined lack of social graces to plain old bad manners. Sometimes, the sabras could even be too prickly for their parents. Older kibbutzniks began to wonder if they had gone too far in trying to free their children from the bonds of polite society, as one kibbutznik explained to Amia Lieblich:

We were . . . revolutionaries; we wanted to liberate ourselves from all the norms and values of the . . . middle class. Man-

doesn't force people to struggle . . . because you receive things, or you don't receive them, independently of your personal efforts. Things just flow, as if by themselves, and one isn't encouraged to initiate any effort . . . or to do anything out of the ordinary. . . . Our school children . . . don't seem to make any attempt to achieve anything. Whatever comes, comes. They want to see immediate results, and won't invest in something that might fail or that will demand a long, ongoing effort. They're very similar to children raised in rich families in town, children who can buy everything, get anything, and therefore never learn to strive, to try, to fail and then succeed.[86]

Community Values, Personal Needs

The Dropouts

Native-born kibbutzniks do not have the political and social commitments that motivated their parents and grandparents. Most sabras who stay on the kibbutz do so because it is home and they love the place; rarely from a sense of duty, or the desire to be part of something larger than themselves. Without the guiding force of ideology, members base their allegiance to the kibbutz on personal satisfaction and quality of life.

Oddly enough, the adventurous spirits who insist on going their own way often retain an almost arrogant pride in their kibbutz origins: "An ex-kibbutznik is easily identified in town," said one dropout.

> Even abroad, people have often recognized me as such. I think we acquire, in the kibbutz, a certain directness of manner, of getting right to the point. We're willing to do any kind of work, we're not choosy. We're not spoiled and can cope with a lot of physical difficulties. We can live on very little, actually. We're simply better than many people I have met in town.[87]

Even on the liberalized kibbutzim, where members have more choices than ever before, a person is still judged by his or her ability to function within the group. Variety and individual expression are fine, so long as they fit within the boundaries of acceptable differences and do not come into open conflict with community standards. For some people, this isn't enough. They crave a kind of intellectual and emotional freedom that cannot exist comfortably on a kibbutz.

It is the nature of collectives to meddle in affairs that would be nobody's business in other societies, and to haggle endlessly over every decision. People who can tolerate this intrusiveness will get along fine, and probably think of themselves as possessing a great deal of personal freedom. People who react by defending their right to choose over their comrades' right to interfere will feel the full weight of public opinion pressing them into a set of standardized behaviors.

In the 1980s, some kibbutzim lost half their membership as more young people opted out of the collective life, trading security for opportunity and adventure in the outside world. A longtime member at Kibbutz Haogen spoke frankly about this problem to Ze'ev Chafets:

The New Work Ethic

Though some people have seen a decline in the work ethic on the modern kibbutz, in The Israelis, *Harry Golden saw a new and broader version of it when he visited Kibbutz Sde Boker, which had built a flourishing community in the heart of the Negev desert.*

"The [founders] of Sde Boker were not animated by a political ideology, they just wanted to farm in the middle of a desert, where it is so hot the visitor can see camels running the other way, looking for water. . . . [The new generation has a different vision:] On the perimeter of Sde Boker stands a collection of colossal statuary, the work of a kibbutznik. That is his job on the kibbutz. . . . Collectively, the kibbutz has decided that politics or art is as useful as harvesting lettuce. Work has become that which provides value for the kibbutz and expression for the worker. . . . [T]he kibbutz can accommodate any aspiration, any creativity."

"Our great failure has been in passing on our values. We believed that the principles of socialism would be transmitted to our children by the fresh air of the kibbutz, just by experiencing this kind of life." She paused, considering all the kibbutz children who have left, including her own son, who is studying in California. Then she sighed. "Sadly, that just isn't true."[88]

Living In, Dropping Out

In addition to people who actually leave the community, there are those who stay in body but leave in spirit. Almost every large kibbutz has a few malcontents who consistently shirk responsibility and do not respond to the usual disciplinary measures. Lieblich quotes one kibbutznik:

[A] big community . . . can allow itself to maintain several good-for-nothings, eternal loafers, in its midst. . . . We even have a term for people of this kind. In kibbutz jargon one says they "carry a yellow ticket." I don't know how this term [began]; it was here before I arrived. A yellow ticket is "given" to a person of whom the society has despaired. It means nobody will put any more pressure on them, nobody will demand that they work or conform . . . [they] should be left alone to do what they want.[89]

"Yellow tickets" are to the kibbutz what town scoundrels and village loafers were to frontier America. They float on the fringes of society, unaware of their marginal status, or at least unconcerned about it. They are allowed to stay partly because the kibbutz feels sorry for them, and partly because nobody knows how to banish them without setting a dangerous precedent.

By definition, membership in a kibbutz is supposed to be for life, and unconditional. When a nonconforming person can be excluded for one set of reasons, what is to prevent other people from being excluded for another set? Most kibbutzim have been unwilling to confront this question, preferring the yellow ticket as a weapon of last resort: "This is a technique adopted by society in order not to reject people. Thus the 'deviants' remain inside, but with a terrible stigma attached to them."[90]

Other unwilling kibbutzniks avoid the stigma, even though they have long since abandoned the ideals that traditionally bind members to the kibbutz and to one another. These "live-in dropouts" pull their own weight in the community, continuing to work and even participate in social life, but they act out of habit rather than commitment. They stay because the prospect of starting over in another place is overwhelming.

Only the Lonely

Single adults face special problems that may keep them in the city even when they would rather go back to the kibbutz. Modern kibbutzim have become strongly family oriented, and unmarried people do not fit the pattern. Those who wish to marry have few opportunities to meet suitable partners. In essence, the kibbutz is a small town where everyone knows everyone else, and the few people who are not paired off are too old, too young, or off limits because they belong to the same *kvutza*.

One young unmarried woman explained the problem that she and others like her

A couple takes an afternoon stroll through Kibbutz Kfar Szold. Kibbutzniks who do not pair off often feel isolated from the larger, family-oriented community.

faced when they tried to return to their home kibbutzim.

> I have met enough ex-kibbutzniks in town to appreciate my kibbutz for what it's worth, but I don't feel I could return alone and go back to the lonely life which I led before. . . . I have my own internal world now and am not afraid of losing it by being caught up in the mediocrity of everyday life. I know that I would be an active member, professionally and emotionally involved. But the basic condition I need is having my own home and family to return to at night when my workday is over. Otherwise I can't return to the kibbutz.[91]

Many kibbutzniks meet their future spouses in the army. Military service for men and women begins right after high school graduation in Israel. For most young kibbutzniks, it is their first real experience of life in the outside world. They are receptive to new relationships, especially romantic ones, but not all of them meet the person they will marry. Those who do not pair off in the military cannot simply go home and slip back into their old lives. The companions of their childhood have scattered, some to the city, some to other kibbutzim. Even those who remain on the kibbutz are often married, and therefore less available to childhood comrades.

In order to keep young adults from leaving the kibbutz in search of a mate, the United Kibbutz Movement and other federations have established marriage bureaus that organize periodic singles-only vacations in kibbutz-owned hotels. These events bring together unmarried kibbutzniks from many different settlements, giving them an opportunity to get acquainted in a relaxed and sociable atmosphere.

Such singles groups are a creative solution to a persistent problem. Kibbutzniks who marry other kibbutzniks are more likely to stay within the movement. Typically, a new couple will spend a year or so on each partner's home kibbutz before deciding which will be their permanent home. During this time of evaluation, both kibbutzim will do their utmost to "win" the young couple. In these days of declining populations, keeping good members and attracting new ones is a matter of survival for many communities.

The Changing Role of Women

Sabra women have not achieved the kind of equality with men that their pioneering mothers and grandmothers had wanted. Freeing women from domesticity proved to be more difficult than anyone thought. As the earliest settlers of Degania discovered, women could live and work as equals with men while the kibbutzim were pioneering settlements of young adults, without children or elderly folk to consider, and with little concern for the ordinary trappings of domesticity: tidy houses, tasty food, pampered children.

By collectivizing these homemaking chores, the early kibbutzniks hoped to free women from their domestic burdens. This ideal of equality worked well with a population of idealists in their twenties who lived in the most spartan style imaginable and worked from dawn to dusk in the fields. When members paired off and started having children, the situation began to change.

In Israel, military service is compulsory for both men and women. While serving their country, many kibbutzniks meet their future spouses.

Before long, men were assigned to work in the fields and factories while women worked in child care or other domestic services. One kibbutz-born sabra explained her dissatisfaction with women's role in the system:

Women in the kibbutz have nowhere to go, they have little choice in life or work. All women know is that between twenty and forty they have to work in child care. . . . I want to study library science in graduate school and to organize our different libraries in a more sensible way. I like to work with books and I prefer helping students find material for their papers rather than teaching them as a group. I know, however, that I have no chance of reaching that position until I'm forty or forty-five years old, and that's a long time to wait. We have several older women who take care of our children's, adult, and foreign-languages libraries. They're not professionals, and the job is

considered a kind of retirement position from the difficult child-care work which younger women must perform.[92]

While many sabra women share this frustration and anger, a growing number are responding in a way that would have shocked their mothers and grandmothers. They decided that if they were going to spend their lives cooking, cleaning, and caring for children, they might as well do it in their own homes.

Criticism of the communal lodging system [for children] was often voiced by women who resented the fact that [so many] of them had to work in child care despite other interests or work preferences. They blamed the system—originally created to establish equality between the sexes and to liberate women from household chores—with enslaving them nevertheless to service in child

Over time, female kibbutzniks have reverted to their traditional domestic roles. A career in child care seems inevitable for most women on the modern kibbutz.

The Country Club Kibbutz

Though life is changing and the kibbutz is challenged as never before, the modern kibbutz has much to recommend it, even for people who measure success by a materialistic standard. Amos Elon described some kibbutz amenities in The Israelis: Founders and Sons.

"Many *kibbutzniks* no longer see themselves as 'workers.' . . . [A] team of researchers asked a number of *kibbutzniks* to what social class they thought they belonged. A third replied, 'the middle class.'

[*Kibbutzniks*] lead healthy, open-air lives in clean, modern, and frequently beautiful surroundings, engulfed by what are probably the largest, greenest, best-tended lawns and flower gardens in the country. . . . Most of the older *kibbutzim* provide recreational facilities comparable to those of an average American country club. Lavishly equipped gymnasiums, swimming pools . . . and tennis courts are available exclusively for residents of *kibbutz* communities that number no more than 1,200 souls."

care, working with "strangers' children" instead of their own.[93]

Somewhat paradoxically, many young mothers complained bitterly about not being allowed a larger role in the lives of their children. As one mother explained, the children's house took away a major source of emotional satisfaction.

Life in the kibbutz is difficult. The showers and toilets we are forced to use are enough to warrant such a statement. But to that must be added the noisy and hurried dining room, the hard work day, the lack of real recreation. We really don't have much, and even for books we must wait in line. All we have left is our children, and we don't even have them, for they are in the children's house. And now they even took *hashkava* (putting the children to bed) away from us. Why? The "experts" say that the parents spoil them when they put them to bed. This may be true, but you have to think of the parents

A mother takes time out of her busy schedule for a bike ride with her children. As the kibbutz continues to change, women try to juggle family responsibilities and community commitments.

sometimes, too, and not always of the children.[94]

While the majority of kibbutz women want an active family life, this does not mean that they want to go back to the total domesticity of their great-grandmothers. Many sabras are trying to juggle home and community responsibilities without giving up the satisfactions of either one. Like their counterparts in America, these women face stress in trying to do justice to both roles, but they also find great satisfaction in developing a lifestyle that is uniquely their own.

Growing Old, Kibbutz Style

One of the biggest challenges to modern kibbutzim is providing for a growing population of aging members. For most of its history, the kibbutz has been a youth-oriented community, with few elderly members needing services. Today that has changed, and the kibbutzim of the 1990s are developing programs to meet the needs of older chaverim.

The result is a plan that is straightforward and simple. Every member has the right to a comfortable retirement within the community, surrounded by relatives, comrades, and friends. The aging parents of members are also eligible for these benefits, whether or not they have ever joined the kibbutz.

Though this may be a heavy burden on community resources, the pioneers made the rule and their descendants have kept it gladly. In Jewish tradition, care for the elderly is a solemn duty. The kibbutz taps its collective resources so that each member can fulfill this duty.

All retirees receive food, housing, clothing, and medical care. In addition to these material necessities, they need never worry about being lonely, isolated, or bored. The

Leaving the Fold

In the changing kibbutz, leaving has become more common, though not much easier. There is still a great deal of emotional conflict associated with the decision, as journalist Ze'ev Chafets discovered when he talked with native-born kibbutzniks Eran and Tizra Netzer. Their conversation is included in Chafets's article "The Longest Goodbye."

"'People once lived on kibbutzim because they wanted to.... Today, members in their 40s and 50s are simply stuck here. They don't leave, but they leave spiritually. To bridge the gap between those who still want to [be socialists] and those who merely want to live in a pleasant village is very difficult.' . . .

I [Chafets] nod in the direction of the small bedroom, where the Netzers' year-old son is asleep. 'Do you think he'll grow up to be a kibbutznik?' I ask.

Eran pauses, but Tizra shakes her head decisively. 'He won't,' she says.

'How do you know?'

She looks at her husband for a long moment, a look of guilty defiance, then she turns to me and says, 'Because within a few months, we're planning to leave. We want to be independent.'"

Caring for the elderly is a solemn duty on the kibbutz. Lifelong members usually remain involved in their communities, providing younger members a living link with kibbutz history.

richly varied life of the community is open to them, and there is always something to do. In this environment, most elderly people remain active and involved long past the usual retirement age.

Elders do not receive, nor do they expect, elaborate courtesies or special privileges. That would be contrary to kibbutz philosophy. They receive the right to live as equals in a community of equals. For most, that means a vital and contented old age.

The presence of active and involved older people has benefited the community as well as the retirees. Outside parents who have lived and worked in many different places with many different kinds of people bring fresh perspectives. Lifelong members bring tradition and a living link with kibbutz history.

Remembrance

Sixty-nine-year-old Asher came to the kibbutz at the age of twenty-two.

> Now that I look back on my life here, I see that I really found the way to realize my dreams: to live by my three principles—being a worker not an employer, cultivating the land, and making my Jewish roots into a national identity. Indeed, lately I visited Germany and met a non-Jewish woman who used to be my friend

At Yad Mordechai, a bronze statue of Mordecai Anielewicz, commander of the Warsaw ghetto revolt, pays tribute to the courageous past of the Jewish people.

before I emigrated. We sat in a coffee shop together and she said: "We all forgot everything, all the dreams of our youth. You are the only one who has lived up to your dreams." I feel very strongly about that, since in my case it isn't the actualization of what I was *educated* to become, but of what I personally discovered to be important.[95]

The history of the kibbutz is a long and honorable one, filled with the stories of real people making real discoveries about their lives. For all its social and economic changes, modern kibbutzniks connect to that history, and take pride in it. Almost every kibbutz has its special place, where kibbutzniks encounter their own history. At Ma'ale Hahamisha, a statue of five young pioneers who died defending the community is the first thing visitors see when they enter the kibbutz. At Yad Mordechai, an enormous bronze of Mordecai Anielewicz, commander of the Warsaw ghetto revolt in World War II, stands before the remains of a bullet-ridden water tank that was destroyed in Israel's 1948 war of independence. In monuments such as these, kibbutzniks and ex-kibbutzniks acknowledge their connection to the past, even while they move forward into a future of change and uncertainty.

The Kibbutz as Social Model

With few exceptions, today's kibbutz is no longer a true socialist collective. There are those who would say that it has strayed too far from its origins and now cannot turn back. Others are not so quick to dismiss the movement that turned a generation of urban Jews into farmers, transformed a wasteland into a homeland, and captured the imagination of the world.

The concept of the kibbutz has inspired a variety of cooperative programs all over the world: Jewish cultural retreats for American young adults, communal farms for Egyptian peasants, youth villages for disadvantaged Israeli children. Each of these programs has adapted kibbutz principles to its special needs, building successful institutions that blend the best of old and new.

United States: Learning to Be Jews

In southern California the Brandeis Collegiate Institute conducts intensive, twenty-six-day encounters with Jewish custom and tradition. The participants are young Jewish adults, college age and older, who are exploring their heritage, and what it has to offer for their lives. The program, originally created in 1939 by Supreme Court justice Louis D. Brandeis and educator Shlomo Bardin, was inspired by three models: "the summer camp; the kibbutz; and the Danish folk high school, a 19th-century innovation that focused on folk culture, a religious sensibility and communal responsibility."[96]

For the duration of each session, participants live together as a community of friends. They start interacting the moment they arrive on the spacious, wooded grounds. In a ritual that would have delighted the pioneers of Degania, each session begins with a dance.

> [New arrivals] have barely had a chance to drop their suitcases and duffel bags when someone directs them toward a covered pavilion where [a dance instructor] nudges them into a circle and asks them to join hands. Within minutes, they've picked up the steps—some of them awkwardly, some with confidence, some looking like they might, perhaps, have wandered into the wrong camp. The group of strangers is suddenly moving in a circle—moving together; as a community of Jews.[97]

In this temporary community participants are free to explore their Jewish identities, and to experience the camaraderie that gave pioneering kibbutzniks their strength and sense of mission.

Egypt: Learning to Be Farmers

A more utilitarian application of kibbutz principles began in 1992, when Egyptian agricultural engineer Muhammad Ibrahim Wali visited Kibbutz Lehavot-Haviva on a fact-finding

At the Brandeis Collegiate Institute in southern California (pictured), participants live and work together in the tradition of the Israeli kibbutz.

mission. His goal—to find out if the kibbutz concept could be adapted to Egyptian needs. Wali was part of a group that planned to establish an experimental cooperative-farming project on the banks of the Nile River. What better model could he study than the kibbutzim of Egypt's closest neighbor?

In his research, Wali decided that the strict collectivism of the kibbutz would not work in Egypt. Egyptians would be uncomfortable in a community where they could not own property or receive payment for their work. "The Egyptian wants to be an owner, a landlord. . . . On a kibbutz, he can't have all this, and it would bother him."[98]

The answer was a cooperative settlement, where people own their homes and land and can grow any crops they choose. They pool resources to market their crops, provide community services, and purchase heavy equipment that none of them could afford to buy alone. In Israel, this type of community is called a *moshav*. Wali thought it would work in Egypt. "We will have to train and prepare [the farmers] for the idea, explain to them what it is all about."[99]

"It Takes a Village to Raise a Child"

As the kibbutzim move away from collective child care, many people in the United States are also grappling with issues that relate to caregiving and the role of women in society. Mary Catherine Bateson discussed these challenges in her essay "Holding Up the Sky Together."

"At present we live in a society that . . . [is] suffering a lack of committed and effective care, ranging from a friendly greeting and a cup of tea at the end of the day to family support at home during illness. The solution proposed by some religious groups is a return to the 'family values' of the 1950s, sending women back to the home. But although there is undoubtedly a need for care, there is no longer any reason to assume it will be provided primarily by women, or in nuclear families, but possibly in cooperative relationships between families or in new businesses and institutions. Indeed, many studies show that children can benefit from half a dozen involved caregivers of both sexes: As the African proverb says, 'It takes a village to raise a child.'"

Undoubtedly, the Egyptian cooperatives will be very different from either Israeli original, which is as it should be. Each innovation will not only change the workaday reality of existing communities, but it will enlarge the concept and keep it responsive to changing needs.

Israel: Learning to Be Good Citizens

As does every nation, Israel has its share of disadvantaged young people, orphaned, emotionally troubled, or living in dysfunctional families. To provide for these children, the government of Israel adapted the principles of the kibbutz to the demands of the situation. The result is the youth village, a cross

The kibbutz continues to inspire modern programs and cooperatives like Israeli youth villages (pictured) that offer disadvantaged young people the chance to live, work, and learn in a communal environment.

between the children's house of the classical kibbutz and an old-fashioned boarding school. In these villages, children at risk find hope, education, and belonging.

The daily schedule of activities is carefully structured to balance school, work, and social life. It begins with a seven o'clock wake-up call followed by morning chores, breakfast, and classes. After school, there is a wide choice of extracurricular activities such as drama, music, or sports. Evening activities often feature lectures or films, which are arranged by a student committee under supervision of a counselor who carries the title of "cultural coordinator." Lights out is 11:30 for high school students, 10:30 for the lower grades.

By the mid-1990s, 45,000 young people lived and studied in 250 youth villages throughout Israel. The program has been so successful that American social workers and educators have begun studying it with a great deal of interest.

"In Israel it works, and it's not so hard to see how it could work in the U.S.," says Dr. Richard English, dean of the Howard University School of Social Work in Washington, D.C., who has observed Israeli facilities firsthand. "Israeli youth villages are places where the individual is valued. They provide a nurturing environment with an educative purpose."[100]

Youth villages, along with other programs that have borrowed from the kibbutz, are part of the legacy that began with Degania in 1909. In the minds of people all over the world the kibbutz continues to stand for deeply human values: cooperation over competition, generosity over greed, the dignity of work. No matter how much its structure and ideology may change over the coming years, that accomplishment has earned an honored place in the history of modern Israel.

Notes

Introduction: A New Way of Living

1. Quoted in Yossi Melman, "Kibbutz: Is the Dream Dead?" *Moment*, vol. 20, no. 1, February 1995, pp. 45–46.
2. Quoted in Ze'ev Chafets, "The Longest Goodbye: Socialism in Israel," *Sacramento Bee Forum*, December 20, 1992, p. 6.

Chapter 1: The First Kibbutz

3. Quoted in Harry Viteles, *A History of the Co-Operative Movement in Israel: A Source Book in 7 Volumes,* vol. 2, *The Evolution of the Kibbutz Movement.* London: Valentine, Mitchell, 1967, pp.38–39.
4. Quoted in Harry Golden, *The Israelis: Portrait of a People.* New York: G. P. Putnam's Sons, 1971, p. 46.
5. Mark Tessler, *A History of the Israeli-Palestinian Conflict.* Indianapolis: Indiana University Press, 1994, p. 64.
6. Quoted in Viteles, *A History of the Co-Operative Movement in Israel,* vol. 2, p. 30.
7. Quoted in Viteles, *A History of the Co-Operative Movement in Israel,* vol. 2, p. 30.
8. Quoted in Viteles, *A History of the Co-Operative Movement in Israel,* vol. 2, p. 39.
9. Quoted in Viteles, *A History of the Co-Operative Movement in Israel,* vol. 2, p. 47.
10. Quoted in Viteles, *A History of the Co-Operative Movement in Israel,* vol. 2, p. 38.
11. Quoted in Viteles, *A History of the Co-Operative Movement in Israel,* vol. 2, p. 39.
12. Quoted in Viteles, *A History of the Co-Operative Movement in Israel,* vol. 2, p. 39.
13. Quoted in Viteles, *A History of the Co-Operative Movement in Israel,* vol. 2, p. 54.

Chapter 2: Work All Day, Dance the Hora All Night

14. Michael Gorkin, *Border Kibbutz.* New York: Grosset & Dunlap, 1971, p. 22.
15. Quoted in Ralph G. Martin, *Golda Meir: The Romantic Years.* New York: Charles Scribner's Sons, 1988, p. 129.
16. Melford E. Spiro, *Kibbutz: Venture in Utopia.* New York: Schocken Books, 1971, p. 19.
17. Amia Lieblich, *Kibbutz Makom: Report from an Israeli Kibbutz.* New York: Pantheon Books, 1981, p. 26.
18. Lieblich, *Kibbutz Makom,* p. 19.
19. Spiro, *Kibbutz: Venture in Utopia,* p. 204.
20. Bruno Bettelheim, *The Children of the Dream.* New York: Macmillan, 1969, p. 250.
21. Gorkin, *Border Kibbutz,* p. 9.
22. Lieblich, *Kibbutz Makom,* p. 30.
23. Lieblich, *Kibbutz Makom,* p. 27.
24. Spiro, *Kibbutz: Venture in Utopia,* pp. 75–76.
25. Quoted in Viteles, *A History of the Co-Operative Movement in Israel,* vol. 2, p. 319.
26. Quoted in Viteles, *A History of the Co-Operative Movement in Israel,* vol. 2, p. 319.
27. Dan Leon, *The Kibbutz: A New Way of Life,* London: Pergamon Press, 1969, pp. 152–53.

28. Spiro, *Kibbutz: Venture in Utopia,* pp. 100–101.
29. Spiro, *Kibbutz: Venture in Utopia,* pp. 89–90.
30. Quoted in Lieblich, *Kibbutz Makom,* p. 79.

Chapter 3: Children of the Dream

31. Quoted in Lieblich, *Kibbutz Makom,* p. 290.
32. Bettelheim, *The Children of the Dream,* p. 88.
33. Bettelheim, *The Children of the Dream,* p. 88.
34. Spiro, *Kibbutz: Venture in Utopia,* pp. 30–31.
35. Golden, *The Israelis,* p. 42.
36. Bettelheim, *The Children of the Dream,* pp. 98–99.
37. Quoted in Bettelheim, *The Children of the Dream,* p. 220.
38. Spiro, *Kibbutz: Venture in Utopia,* pp. 134–35.
39. Quoted in Lieblich, *Kibbutz Makom,* p. 172.
40. Leon, *The Kibbutz,* p. 107.
41. Leon, *The Kibbutz,* p. 108.
42. Quoted in Gorkin, *Border Kibbutz,* p. 173.
43. Spiro, *Kibbutz: Venture in Utopia,* p. 138.
44. Spiro, *Kibbutz: Venture in Utopia,* p. 138.
45. Bettelheim, *The Children of the Dream,* pp. 204–205.
46. Bettelheim, *The Children of the Dream,* pp. 213–14.

Chapter 4: The Kibbutz and Its Arab Neighbors

47. Quoted in Viteles, *A History of the Co-Operative Movement in Israel,* vol. 2, p. 38.
48. Tessler, *A History of the Israeli-Palestinian Conflict,* pp. 64–65.
49. Tessler, *A History of the Israeli-Palestinian Conflict,* p. 183.
50. Danny Rubinstein, *The People of Nowhere: The Palestinian Vision of Home.* New York: Times Books, 1991, p. 81.
51. Quoted in Rubinstein, *The People of Nowhere,* p. 81.
52. Quoted in Rubinstein, *The People of Nowhere,* p. 42.
53. Rubinstein, *The People of Nowhere,* p. 45.
54. Rubinstein, *The People of Nowhere,* pp. 46–47.
55. Gorkin, *Border Kibbutz,* p. 90.
56. Quoted in Gorkin, *Border Kibbutz,* p. 91.
57. Quoted in Lieblich, *Kibbutz Makom,* pp. 61–62.
58. Amos Elon, *The Israelis: Founders and Sons.* New York: Holt, Rinehart & Winston, 1971, p. 239.
59. Quoted in Elon, *The Israelis,* pp. 240–41.
60. David K. Shipler, *Arab and Jew: Wounded Spirits in a Promised Land.* New York: Penguin Books, 1986, p. 114.
61. Quoted in Shipler, *Arab and Jew,* p. 115.
62. Quoted in David Grossman, *Sleeping on a Wire: Conversations with Palestinians in Israel.* New York: Farrar, Straus & Giroux, 1993, p. 145.
63. Quoted in Shipler, *Arab and Jew,* pp. 207–208.

Chapter 5: The New Kibbutz: A Community in Transition

64. Spiro, *Kibbutz: Venture in Utopia,* pp. 64–65.
65. Chafets, "The Longest Goodbye," p. 6.
66. Chafets, "The Longest Goodbye," p. 6.
67. Quoted in Lieblich, *Kibbutz Makom,* p. 29.
68. Spiro, *Kibbutz: Venture in Utopia,* pp. 166–67.

69. Hazael Toledano, "The Kibbutz in Crisis," *World Press Review*, October 1992, p. 46.

70. Quoted in Chafets, "The Longest Good-bye," p. 1.

71. Clyde Haberman, "Reluctantly, a Kibbutz Turns to (Gasp!) the Stock Market," *The New York Times*, July 8, 1993, p. A1.

72. Quoted in Haberman, "Reluctantly, a Kibbutz Turns . . . ," p. A1.

73. Quoted in Lieblich, *Kibbutz Makom*, p. 9.

74. Melman, "Kibbutz: Is the Dream Dead?" p. 51.

75. Quoted in Toledano, "The Kibbutz in Crisis," p. 46.

76. Quoted in Chafets, "The Longest Good-bye," p. 1.

77. Quoted in Lieblich, *Kibbutz Makom*, p. 247.

78. A. I. Rabin and Benjamin Beit-Hallahmi, *Twenty Years Later: Kibbutz Children Grown Up.* New York: Springer, 1982, p. 195.

79. Quoted in Lieblich, *Kibbutz Makom*, p. 214.

80. Melman, "Kibbutz: Is the Dream Dead?" p. 51.

81. Quoted in Haberman, "Reluctantly, a Kibbutz Turns . . . ," p. A6.

82. Quoted in Melman, "Kibbutz: Is the Dream Dead?" pp. 88–89.

83. Quoted in Haberman, "Reluctantly, a Kibbutz Turns . . . ," p. B10.

Chapter 6: Community Values, Personal Needs

84. Golden, *The Israelis*, p. 23.

85. Quoted in Lieblich, *Kibbutz Makom*, p. 38.

86. Quoted in Lieblich, *Kibbutz Makom*, p. 289.

87. Quoted in Lieblich, *Kibbutz Makom*, p. 276.

88. Quoted in Chafets, "The Longest Good-bye," p. 6.

89. Quoted in Lieblich, *Kibbutz Makom*, p. 256.

90. Quoted in Lieblich, *Kibbutz Makom*, p. 256.

91. Quoted in Lieblich, *Kibbutz Makom*, pp. 276–77.

92. Quoted in Lieblich, *Kibbutz Makom*, p. 104.

93. Quoted in Lieblich, *Kibbutz Makom*, p. 313.

94. Quoted in Spiro, *Kibbutz: Venture in Utopia*, p. 232.

95. Quoted in Lieblich, *Kibbutz Makom*, p. 246.

Conclusion: The Kibbutz as Social Model

96. Thomas Fields-Meyer, "When Generation X Asks 'Why?'" *Moment*, June 1995, p. 29.

97. Fields-Meyer, "When Generation X Asks 'Why?' p. 28.

98. Quoted in Amir Gilat, "A Model for Egypt?" *World Press Review*, October 1992, p. 46.

99. Quoted in Gilat, "A Model for Egypt?" p. 46.

100. Quoted in Cynthia Mann, "Bring Back the Orphanage? Israel Has a Better Idea," *Moment*, June 1995, p. 32.

For Further Reading

Josh Clayton-Felt, *To Be Seventeen in Israel.* New York: Franklin Watts, 1987. This teen's eye view of Israel shows the influence of group values on Israeli culture outside the kibbutz.

Amos Elon, *The Israelis: Founders and Sons.* New York: Holt, Rinehart & Winston, 1971. Readable history of Israel, through the eyes of individuals rather than from the perspective of political institutions. Includes excellent look at the kibbutzim.

Ellen Frankel, *The Classic Tales: 4000 Years of Jewish Lore.* Northvale, NJ: Jason Aronson, 1989. Retellings of myth, legend, fable, and allegory from the long Jewish tradition. Captures the spirit and the cultural wisdom of the people who created the kibbutz.

Harry Golden, *The Israelis: Portrait of a People.* New York: G. P. Putnam's Sons, 1971. A highly personal look at Israeli life by a Jewish-American author known for peppering his work with vivid, often humorous, anecdotes.

Michael Gorkin, *Border Kibbutz.* New York: Grosset & Dunlap, 1971. The experiences of an American writer researching a book at a kibbutz that lived under constant threat of attack from hostile neighbors.

Peter Hay, *Ordinary Heroes: The Life and Death of Chana Szenes, Israel's National Heroine.* New York: Paragon House, 1989. The inspiring story of a young kibbutznik who gave her life in World War II, trying to save Jews from the Nazis. Includes good descriptions of Chana's life on the kibbutz.

Peter Hellman, *Heroes: Tales from the Israeli Wars.* New York: Henry Holt, 1990. A look at war in modern Israel, through the eyes of ordinary soldiers. Includes the wartime experiences of kibbutzniks.

Amia Lieblich, *Kibbutz Makom: Report from an Israeli Kibbutz.* New York: Pantheon Books, 1981. An in-depth study of one kibbutz; its formation, traditions, and difficulties.

Amos Oz, *In the Land of Israel.* New York: Harcourt Brace Jovanovich, 1983. One of Israel's best writers, a longtime kibbutznik and peace activist, looks at the strife in his homeland.

Works Consulted

Nathan Ausubel, *The Book of Jewish Knowledge*. New York: Crown, 1964. An alphabetic overview of Jewish history and knowledge, from biblical times to the present.

Nathan Ausubel, ed., *A Treasury of Jewish Folklore*. New York: Crown, 1948. Jewish legends, folktales, and songs from many sources.

Mary Catherine Bateson, "Holding Up the Sky Together," *Civilization*, May/June 1995. Discusses the need for cooperation and partnership between men and women.

Alex Bein, *Theodore Hertzl: A Biography*. London: East and West Library, 1957. Definitive biography of the founder of modern political Zionism.

Bruno Bettelheim, *The Children of the Dream*. New York: Macmillan, 1969. An American authority on child development studies the psychological effects of growing up on a kibbutz.

Ze'ev Chafets, "The Longest Goodbye: Socialism in Israel," *Sacramento Bee Forum*, December 20, 1992. A look at how the decline of world socialism has affected life on the kibbutz.

Thomas Fields-Meyer, "When Generation X Asks Why?" *Moment*, June 1995. A behind-the-scenes look at an American program for Jewish young adults based upon principles of the kibbutzim.

Amir Gilat, "A Model for Egypt?" *World Press Review*, October 1992. A vivid description of efforts to adapt the Israeli kibbutz to the needs of Egyptian farmers.

David Grossman, *Sleeping on a Wire: Conversations with Palestinians in Israel*. New York: Farrar, Straus & Giroux, 1993. A Jewish writer's sensitive look at the plight of Palestinians.

Clyde Haberman, "Reluctantly, a Kibbutz Turns to (Gasp!) the Stock Market," *The New York Times*, July 8, 1993. Inroads of capitalism in the kibbutz economy.

Hertzl Press, *Zionism: A Basic Reader*. New York: Hertzl Press, 1975. A selection of writings by Jews and non-Jews relating to the topic of Zionism.

Rabbi Morris N. Kertzner, *What Is a Jew?* Rev. ed. New York: Macmillan, 1974. A question-and-answer approach to Jewish traditions and belief.

Dan Leon, *The Kibbutz: A New Way of Life*. London: Pergamon Press, 1969. An inside look at the philosophy and lifestyle of "classic" kibbutzim.

Cynthia Mann, "Bring Back the Orphanage? Israel Has a Better Idea," *Moment*, June 1995. A fascinating look at Israeli youth villages, which provide live-in education for disadvantaged children.

Ralph G. Martin, *Golda Meir: The Romantic Years*. New York: Charles Scribner's Sons, 1988. A biography of the late Israeli prime minister, a former kibbutznik.

Yossi Melman, "Kibbutz: Is the Dream Dead?" *Moment*, February 1995. The new commercialism on the kibbutz.

A. I. Rabin and Benjamin Beit-Hallahmi, *Twenty Years Later: Kibbutz Children Grown Up*. New York: Springer, 1982. A follow-up study of kibbutz-born sabras as young adults.

Norman Rose, *Chaim Weizmann: A Biography*. New York: Viking Penguin, 1986. The biography of Israel's first president reveals a great deal about the early years of statehood, including the pioneering kibbutzim.

Danny Rubinstein, *The People of Nowhere: The Palestinian Vision of Home*. New York: Times Books, 1991. An Israeli journalist examines the Palestinian point of view with compassion and fairness.

Tom Segev, *The Seventh Million: The Israelis and the Holocaust*. New York: Hill and Wang, 1993. A sensitive examination of how survivors of Nazi death camps fared in Israel.

David K. Shipler, *Arab and Jew: Wounded Spirits in a Promised Land*. New York: Penguin Books, 1986. Takes a detailed look at the schism between the two peoples who call Palestine home.

Melford E. Spiro, *Kibbutz: Venture in Utopia*. New York: Schocken Books, 1971. A perceptive evaluation of the development of the kibbutz and its contributions to Israeli society.

Mark Tessler, *A History of the Israeli-Palestinian Conflict*. Indianapolis: Indiana University Press, 1994. A study of both sides in the decades-long conflict, with special emphasis on the peace process.

Hazael Toledano, "The Kibbutz in Crisis," *World Press Review*, October 1992. A look at the mounting debt crisis that was the result of the free-spending 1980s.

Harry Viteles, *A History of the Co-Operative Movement in Israel: A Source Book in 7 Volumes*. London: Valentine, Mitchell, 1966–1970. A detailed sourcebook that draws from primary sources to chronicle the development of Israeli socialism.

Index

adolescent rebellion, 44
agriculture, 8-9, 14
allowance, 64
Always Kibbutz, 69
Anielewicz, Mordecai, 80
Arab and Jew: Wounded Spirits in a Promised Land (Shipler), 54, 56
Arabs, Palestinian, 47
  exile of, 49-51
  Jews and
    cultural differences between, 55-57
    relations between, 48-49
Ashdot Ya'acov, 46
Ausubel, Nathan, 15, 62
Aviel, Saul, 69

Baratz
  Joseph, 48
  Miriam, 15
bar/bat mitzvah, 42
barhash, 20-21
Bateson, Mary C., 82
Bedouins, 56
Beit Ha-Gefen, 55
Beit-Hallahmi, Benjamin, 29
Beit Oren, 67
Bettelheim, Bruno, 23, 35, 37, 44, 45
The Bible, 41
The Book of Jewish Knowledge (Ausubel), 15, 62

Brandeis, Louis D., 81
Brandeis Collegiate Institute, 81
Bussel, Joseph, 12

capitalism, 67
Chafets, Ze'ev, 78
chamseen, 20
child rearing
  changes in, 65-66
  in Degania, 16-17
  kindergarten years, 38
  toddlers, 36-37
children, 41
The Children of the Dream (Bettelheim), 35
Children's Community, 38-40, 42
civil defense, 51-52
climate, 13-14, 20
crops, 14
cultural activities, 29-30

dating, 43
Dayan, Yaël, 10
Degania, 11, 12
  child rearing in, 16-17
  hiring of outside workers in, 13
  legacy of, 19
  living conditions in, 14
  membership in, 17
  and non-Jewish laborers, 47-48
  women's roles, 15-17
dining hall, 25-26

demise of, 63-64
dropouts, 72-73

eastern Europe, 9, 11
Ein Zivan, 66
elderly
  care of, 78-79
Elon, Amos, 53, 77
English, Richard, 83
ezra hadadit (mutual aid), 12, 22

factories, 64
festivals, 30

general assembly, 24
Goldberger, Meream, 10
Golden, Harry, 36, 70, 72
Gorkin, Michael, 25, 42, 51, 52
governing, 23-25
Grossman, David, 55

Hadash, Shmuel, 10
Hakibbutz Hadati, 20, 67
Hakibbutz Hameuchad, 67
Hebrew, 19
Hellman, Peter, 37
Heros: Tales from the Israeli Wars (Hellman), 37
high school, 42-43
"Holding Up the Sky Together" (Bateson), 82
hora (dance), 14
Hussein ibn Talal (King of Jordan), 57

Ichud Hakvutzut
  Vehakibbutzim, 67
individuality, 45
industrialization, 61
Israel
  creation of, 49
*The Israelis: Founders and
  Sons* (Elon), 53, 77
The Israelis (Golden), 70,
  72

Jewish heritage, learning
  about, 41
Jewish National Fund, 11,
  13

*The Kibbutz: A New Way of
  Life* (Leon), 16
Kibbutz: Venture in Utopia
  (Spiro), 24, 31
Kibbutz Bilat, 51
Kibbutzim
  changes in, 59-66
  opposition to, 50-52
  origins of, 11
  way of life, 8-10
Kibbutz Makom (Lieblich),
  31, 40
Kibbutz Sa'ad
"kibbutz salad," 25
kindergarten, 38
Kinneret, 62
Kiryat Yedidim, 58-59
kitat maavar (transition
  class), 38
kvutza, 11, 24, 37, 45, 71

labor
  division of, 27
  non-Jewish, 47

in Degania, 13
land
  Arab versus Jewish bond
    with, 50-51
  ownership of, 21
  reclaiming, in Degania,
    13
Lehavot-Haviva, 81-82
Leon, Dan, 16, 40, 41
Lieblich, Amia, 35, 40, 65,
  71
living conditions
  in Degania, 14
  in modern kibbutzim, 8
"The Longest Goodbye"
  (Chafets), 78

Ma'ale Hahamisha, 61, 80
malaria, 20
Malkin, Yaacov
marriage, 74
Meir, Golda, 20
Melman, Yossi, 10, 69
metapelet (care-giver), 34,
  35
military service, 53, 74
Misgav Am, 54
moshav, 82
My Father, His Daughter
  (Dayan), 10

Near, Henry, 69
Neot Mordechai, 64
newborns, 34

Palestine, 9
  return of Jews to, 11
  settlements in, 1855-1914,
    11
Palestine Liberation

Organization (PLO), 57
Palestinian Arabs, 47
  exile of, 49-51
  Jews and
    cultural differences
      between, 55-57
    relations between,
      48-49
Passover, 30, 31
The People of Nowhere
  (Rubinstein), 49
p'kak (substitute worker),
  27-28
PLO (Palestine Liberation
  Organization), 57
pogrom (mass murder), 9,
  11
privacy, 23
private enterprise, 61-63
property rights, 21, 22

Rabin, Yitzhak (Israeli
  prime minister), 57
Rabin, A.I., 29
recreation, 29-30
Rosner, Menachem, 67
Rubinstein, Danny, 49, 50
Russia, 9, 11

Sabbath ("day of rest"), 30,
  68
  kibbutz routine and, 19
sabra, 70-71
schools
  changes in, 65-66
  extracurricular activities,
    43
Secretariat (executive
  council), 24, 30
Seder (Passover ceremony),

31
Shipler, David, 54, 56
single adults, 73-75
Six-Day War of 1967, 53, 55
socialism, 62-63
  vs. capitalism, 67
socialists, 11, 22
Spiro, Melford E., 21, 24, 27, 31, 43, 58, 59
Succoth, 30
suicide, 32-33
Sziselman, Daniel, 64-65

teachers, 40
teenagers
  adolescent rebellion and, 44-45
  social life of, 43-44

terrorism, 53-54
Tessler, Mark, 13, 48
Twain, Mark, 18
Twenty Years Later: Kibbutz Children Grow Up (Beit-Hallahmi and Rabin), 29

Um Elfahm, 55
Um Juni, 12, 15
United Kibbutz Movement, 66-67, 74
United Nations, 49

vacations, 28-29

Wali, Muhammad Ibrahim, 81-82
women, roles of, 27

changes in, 75-78
  at Degania, 15-17
workers
  rights and responsibilities of, 28
  status of, 62
work ethic, 72

Yad Mordechai, 80
"yellow tickets," 73
Yemenites, 17-18
Yiddish, 19
Yishuv (Jewish community), 19

Zionism: A Basic Reader, 18
Zionism, meaning of, 15
Zionists, 11

Picture Credits

Cover photo: © Ted Spiegel

AP/Wide World Photos, Inc., 30, 41, 50, 51

Archive Photos, 20, 27, 52, 75

© ASAP/Israel Talby/Woodfin Camp & Associates, Inc., 63, 65, 66, 74, 83

© Aliza Auerbach/ASAP/Woodfin Camp & Associates, Inc., 74

The Bettmann Archive, 17, 32, 56

© Lev Borodulin/ASAP/Woodfin Camp & Associates, Inc., 46, 60, 61, 80

Brandeis-Bardin Institute, 82

© CZA/ASAP/Woodfin Camp & Associates, Inc., 13, 14

Embassy of Israel, 28, 38

© Olivia Heussler/Impact Visuals, 79

© Avi Hirschfield/ASAP/Woodfin Camp & Associates, Inc., 70, 76

Hulton Deutsch Collection Limited, 9, 21, 23, 35, 39 (bottom), 43, 45

Israel Ministry of Tourism, 8, 58

© Hilary Marcus/Impact Visuals, 36, 68, 77

North Wind Picture Archives, 18

© Richard Nowitz/ASAP/Woodfin Camp & Associates, Inc., 25

Reuters/Bettmann Archive, 57

UPI/Bettmann Newsphotos, 33, 48, 53

Yad Tabenkin Archives, 26, 34, 39 (top), 44

About the Author

Linda Jacobs Altman has written many books for children and young people, including *Amelia's Road*, the story of a young migrant farmworker, and *Genocide: The Systematic Killing of a People*. Her interest in the kibbutz began when she visited Kibbutz Ma'ale Hahamisha during a research trip to Israel.

She lives with her husband, Richard, and an assortment of four-legged friends in Clearlake, California. When not writing she enjoys studying Spanish and collecting VHS movies.